Status of Adivasis/Indigenous Peoples Mining Series – 3

ANDHRA PRADESH

DISCLAIMER

The author and the editorial collective are solely responsible for the contents of this report. The views expressed in this report do not necessarily reflect the views of institutions who supported the research nor who supported printing.

Status of Adivasis/Indigenous
Peoples Mining Series – 3

ANDHRA PRADESH

Patrik Oskarsson

A Status of Adivasis/Indigenous Peoples Mining Series – 3 :
ANDHRA PRADESH

Patrik Oskarsson

First Published, 2014

ISBN 978-93-5002-283-2

Published by
AAKAR BOOKS
28 E Pocket IV, Mayur Vihar Phase I, Delhi 110 091
Phone: 011 2279 5505 Telefax: 011 2279 5641
aakarbooks@gmail.com; www.aakarbooks.com

In association with
THE OTHER MEDIA
J 139, First Floor, Vikas Puri
New Delhi 110 018
Phones: 011 2854 3372/73, Fax: 011 4237 1129
Email: tom@theothermedia.org

Printed at
Saurabh Printers Pvt. Ltd., A 16, Sector IV, Noida

Acknowledgements

The Status of Adivasis/Indigenous Peoples (SAIP) has been an important initiative of The Other Media and All India Coordinating Forum of Adivasis/Indigenous Peoples. It began with a lot of interest and enthusiasm with a wide consultation among activists, scholars and researchers interested in Adivasis/Indigenous People's issues. However, the process seemed to have had its own pace and could not keep up with the expectation of completing the report on time. The present phase of the programme has covered, state-wise, issues of land and mining in the Adivasis/Indigenous People's areas.

This report on mining issues in the Adivasi areas of Meghalaya has been prepared by Gideon L Kharkongor and Rajesh Dutta. Members of the EC went through the report and gave their valuable comments and suggestions. We gratefully acknowledge their contribution that was available at every stage of preparation of the report. The efforts of the EC have been untiringly coordinated by C R Bijoy. The reports owe a lot to his relentless efforts to keep in the loop everyone concerned towards producing good results out of the reports. At the level of The Other Media, Ravi Hemadri, who worked as the Executive Director of the organisation through most part of the programme serves as a link between the organisation and the EC. He continued to coordinate the final editing and printing of the reports. We gratefully acknowledge the role played by both C R Bijoy and Ravi Hemadri.

We acknowledge and thank the Adivasi Academy, Tejgarh, Gujarat, and particularly Prof Ganesh Devy, for generously hosting in February 2008, a two-day workshop of members of the EC and authors to review the draft reports. We thank the members of the Advisory Board of the SAIP, who with their participation in the first consultation and later whenever called upon, gave their inputs to the reports. Thanks are due to Shankar Gopalakrishnan who meticulously put together statistical data and selected literature for SAIP.

Finally we would like to acknowledge and thank our funders ICCO, Netherlands, and TROCAIRE, Ireland, who supported the programme right through the last five years. We are grateful to the Foundation for Ecological Security, Anand, Gujarat, and OXFAM who generously supported the printing of the first phase of reports on Mining. We thank all of them for being patient with this initiative.

E Deenadayalan
General Secretary

Contents

List of Tables and Figures

Tables

Figures

Glossary and Acronyms

Alumina	A white powder consisting of aluminium oxide. Mainly used to produce aluminium metal.
AP	Andhra Pradesh
APIIC	Andhra Pradesh Industrial Infrastructure Corporation, a Government of Andhra Pradesh company responsible for industrial development.
APMDC	Andhra Pradesh Mineral Development Corporation, a Government of Andhra Pradesh company.
APSLTR	The Andhra Pradesh Scheduled Area Land Transfer Regulation 1959 as amended up to 1970. Also known as the 1/70 Act, the First Act of 1970.
Bauxite	An ore containing aluminium oxide (alumina), and a range of other elements. The ore is refined in two stages to first produce alumina and later the metal aluminium.
EIA	Environmental Impact Assessment
Gram Panchayat	Assembly of elected local (village) officials.
Gram Sabha	Assembly of all adults within the area of a Panchayat to allow for direct democracy.
ITDA	Integrated Tribal Development Agency, welfare offices operating in the Scheduled Areas of Andhra Pradesh under the State Tribal Welfare Department.
JSW	Jindal South West Ltd., a subsidiary to the OP Jindal Group.

GoAP	Government of Andhra Pradesh
GoI	Government of India
Mandal	Block, Tehsil, smaller administrative unit of a District
MoEF	Ministry of Environment and Forests, Union Government
Panchayat	Lowest unit of the three-tier system of local democratic institutions across India. The others are Block (Mandal) and District Councils.
Patta	Land title
Project Affected Families	Families defined according to AP Government R & R policies as having a right to compensation but not rehabilitation. Usually this is due to them losing agricultural land but not the house.
Project Displaced Families	Families defined according to AP Government R & R policies as having a right to compensation including rehabilitation.
PESA	Panchayat (Extension to Scheduled Areas) Act, an act to modify and implement local self-governance in the Scheduled Areas across India.
R & R	Resettlement and Rehabilitation (of people displaced from land acquisition).
Scheduled Areas	The Scheduled Areas are areas notified by the President of India under the Fifth Schedule of the Constitution. These are tribal-dominated areas.
Scheduled Castes	These are notified by the President of India for being historically-disadvantaged people. They are also popularly called Dalits.
Scheduled Tribes	These are notified by the President of India for being historically-disadvantaged people. They are also popularly called Adivasis/tribal peoples.

Preface

Eighty-eight million Adivasis and indigenous peoples live in India—approximately one-fourth of the world's total indigenous population. Historically self-sufficient, forest-based communities with independent cultural identities, they have been subjected to displacement, dispossession and repression for more than a century and are now India's poorest and most marginalised communities. Since the onset of British rule, and in many cases from much earlier, Adivasis and indigenous peoples have been systematically and forcibly dispossessed of the resources of their homelands. In gross violation of democratic practice, social justice and both constitutional and legal requirements, such dispossession continues to this day. It is also the Adivasis and indigenous peoples who have paid the heaviest price for the current neo-liberal globalisation policies, with their land, resources and forests taken from them for private capital in the name of "economic growth."

These larger processes have been accompanied by the erosion and undermining of cultural identities, leading to a loss of cultural moorings and other markers of ethnicity. Less than half of India's Adivasi communities speak their own language. State and private efforts at "mainstreaming" and against indigenous faiths, practices and cultural mores have had a devastating impact.

Such trends have not gone unchallenged. Despite

growing differentiation, ethnicity has emerged as a strong, consolidating force. Many have organised, often with the help of sympathetic outsiders, to fight against their oppressors and struggle for the control over land and other resources, and for local self-government as in parts of central India. There have been demands for political self-determination and autonomy of varying degrees as in Jharkhand and the north-east. The state characterises all such struggles as 'Law and Order Problems', and large parts of central India and the north-east are heavily militarised in the name of 'national security'. In other parts too state repression has been heavy and brutal.

Though these processes are well-known to many and particularly to Adivasis and indigenous peoples' movements, there continues to be a dearth of knowledge on the overall status of Adivasis and indigenous peoples in India. The struggle-based mass organisations of Adivasis and indigenous peoples in the Indian subcontinent articulated the need to work towards such a task in the late 1990s. The collective process to fulfil this task was launched in 2005.

The Status of Adivasis/Indigenous Peoples is conceptualised as a series of reports on salient themes affecting the lives of Adivasis/Indigenous Peoples. In the first instance, the series focuses on the situation of land and mining in the tribal tracts of the country. We hope that the series will be effective in not only deliberating on similar themes of importance to the Adivasi present and future, but also help strengthening linkages amongst movements, activists, scholars and all others who are concerned with the protection of the rights of Adivasis/Indigenous Peoples in the Indian subcontinent.

This series of reports will explore the history, the laws, and the facts, and describe struggles while providing an overview of current realities. The main purpose of these reports is to expand linkages and relationships between movements, scholars, and activists so that the future of the political struggles is informed and forward looking.

Executive Summary

The hilly and forested regions of northern Andhra Pradesh are the main areas inhabited by Adivasis in the state. Over 5 million tribals live bordering India's main central tribal regions. The Adivasi areas remain far behind in terms of human development despite Andhra Pradesh on average being much better than most other states with large Adivasi populations. Adivasi areas are also increasingly the target of mining companies despite strict laws banning private mining and industry as well as strong civil society protests.

Andhra Pradesh is a major coal mining state, second only to Jharkhand while standing first in terms of value of production. The state is also the biggest in minor mineral production. Mining has more than doubled in size since the 1990s and further expansions continue to be made. There is a great overlap between the Adivasi areas and the existence of especially coal and bauxite ore deposits, but also of limestone, in the state.

A long history of Adivasi struggles continues to offer protection to Adivasis however. The transfer of tribal land is regulated by very strong state land transfer laws which along with the Supreme Court Samatha Judgement of 1997 constitute a supportive legal frame which prohibits the transfer of non-tribal and state land to non-tribals including private mining companies. However, public sector companies are free to access and take over the land and this has benefited particularly the public sector coal mining company Singareni Colleries which operates an increasing number of open cast coal mines in the Telangana region and in large part on Adivasi land.

The process of alienation of Adivasis and denial of their customary rights to land, forests and waters, have led to large-scale disaffection. The region has been known to be the hotbed of left wing extremists though this is less the case nowadays. Loss of forests, destruction of water sources, pollution, loss of land to cultivation and land alienation due to mining are serious. Bauxite mining has especially become an issue which political parties cannot afford to ignore and movements continue to bring it to attention. Increasing attention to problems caused by mining and supportive legislation can thus provide reasons for cautious hope for improved future rights for Adivasis in Andhra Pradesh.

1

Introduction

In Andhra Pradesh, as elsewhere in India, it is the hilly, forested regions mainly inhabited by Adivasis which are increasingly being targeted by mining companies. The overwhelming majority of the 5 million Adivasis in Andhra Pradesh live in the northern parts of the state bordering India's main central tribal regions.[1] The main Adivasi belt of northern Andhra Pradesh could geographically and geologically be said to, in many ways, belong more to the large central Adivasi areas rather than to a south Indian state. Sadly, the poverty of the people is also more along the lines of central India rather than the somewhat better off plains of Andhra Pradesh. Where the state, although with significant inequalities, has made improvements in human development in recent years, the Adivasi areas remain far behind on commonly used human development indicators. For example, the infant mortality rate is 120-150 for Adivasis compared to 72 for the rest of the state. There is a 30% mortality rate for under fives, which for some Adivasi groups like Savara and Gadaba of coastal AP, go up to over 50%. Additionally it was shown that 65% of Adivasi children age 1-5 suffer from malnutrition, and only about half of all

1. There are, however, areas inhabited by tribal people elsewhere in the state as well as a couple of tribes which have always based themselves outside the Scheduled Areas.

households consumed adequate amounts of protein and energy according to a survey in Khammam District.[2] In terms of education, Adivasis in Andhra Pradesh (AP) have remained as excluded as they have from healthcare. In 2001, 37% of tribals were recorded as literate, with the rate for women being 26%. The Dalit literacy rate in AP was 60.5% as a comparison.[3]

There is a great overlap between the tribal areas in the north and the existence of especially coal and bauxite ore, but also of limestone. The main coal belt today mined by public sector Singareni Colleries runs along the Godavari river valley through the district of Adilabad, Warangal, Karimnagar and Khammam, all in Telangana. In terms of area, impact and sheer scale of mining, coal is much larger than anything else operating in the state. Andhra Pradesh is also, from a national point of view, a major coal mining state, second only to Jharkhand in terms of annual production. Coal mining being totally in the public sector, and with a long history of operations, has allowed it to carry on its activities irrespective of the ban on non-tribal mining. A slow shift away from underground mining and towards open cast has reduced employment opportunities and increased displacement as well as overall environmental degradation in recent years. Despite this, it is only in recent years that larger protests have been organised related to this form of mining compared to especially bauxite mining which has seen significant opposition at least since the 1990s.

1.1 Mining Statistics

Mining has been on the increase in Andhra Pradesh in recent years more than doubling the value of production from 1997-98 to 2004-05. In 2006, there were 1,482 mines operating in the state over an area of 206,250 hectares. This large area, still however only accounted for 0.75% of the total area of

2. Laxmaiah et al., 2007.
3. Office of the Registrar General, India, 2001.

the state. The largest share of land used for mining comes from limestone mines which occupy 46% of the total area under mining.[4] Limestone mining is however only partially carried out in the adivasi areas and therefore not covered more than briefly in this report.

In 2004-2005, Rs. ,200 crore worth of minerals were mined in the state making Andhra Pradesh the biggest mining state in the country in terms of value of production. This is mainly due to the state's large coal mines which accounted for 56% of total value. Despite significant limestone mining, this only accounted for 4% of mineral value, possibly since limestone is usually mined by cement companies and therefore not openly sold on the market. Andhra Pradesh is, however, also the biggest among minor minerals mining which includes sand, marble and similar non-metallic minerals. AP was even larger than Rajasthan which has been traditionally recognised in minor minerals. In metallic minerals, such as iron, bauxite or manganese, AP does not even figure among the top 8 states of the country although plans to expand iron and bauxite mining might change this in the future. In terms of royalty, it is only Jharkhand which earned more in 2004-05, while Andhra Pradesh earned Rs. 864.5 crores, or about 3% of the state revenue receipts. It is well-known that there is no mechanism to distribute the income back to the areas where mining is taking place to compensate for the many additional costs they will have to bear in terms of changes to environment and water. What this also shows however is low importance of mining royalty in the state budget. Even a large mining state like Odisha does not earn more than 5-6% of its budget from mining royalties.[5]

1.2 Special Legal Protection

In a state strongly promoting industrialisation, the impoverished minority of Adivasis could be expected to

---

4. Bhushan and Zeya-Hazra, 2008.
5. Bhushan and Zeya-Hazra, 2008.

come out on the losing side every time, given its remote location and the persisting deep poverty. This being mainly the case, some successes do exist however. The Supreme Court Samatha Judgement in 1997, which so far has only been implemented in the state of Andhra Pradesh, and continued civil society mobilisation has been surprisingly successful at keeping large-scale private mining away from the Scheduled Areas, while finding it harder to counter the many smaller mines, for example gems or sand, which can appear from one day to the next in an area and then quickly disappear again. The key to mining, like many other activities where outsiders come to exploit the natural resources of tribal areas, remain the AP State Land Transfer Regulation 1970, the so called 1/70 Act, which bans any transfer of land including leasing of so-called government owned land and forest to non-tribals. Seen together with the Samatha Judgement, which called for a tribal share in profits and decision-making, the basic building blocks of Adivasi self-rule over mineral resources are present in the law. But not only is there a great need to implement these in order to ensure Adivasi rights over economic development and control over natural resources but they would also need to be expanded to many other activities including those undertaken by the government in areas other than mining and industry such as tourism, coffee and forest plantations.

Cross-cutting the Scheduled Areas and the issue of private land rights for tribal people is the issue of vast stretches of forest mainly in the Scheduled Areas which since long has been settled as government land despite forest-dwellers living and depending on this land for generations. When mining is proposed, a new injustice is committed when official planning considers only how forest loss should be compensated elsewhere, and not the displacement which is often taking place on the ground. In recent years, attempts to open up further mines in tribal areas is going on at the same time as the tribal Forest Rights Act is under implementation to secure legally recognised *pattas* for the first time in history (see bauxite mining chapter). Another process has been the increasing use of afforestation schemes, where first displacement occurs from, for example, a coal mine, and then new displacement for afforestation (see coal mining chapter).

When increased mining in other Adivasi areas of the country often tend to be blamed on the entry of multinational corporations, the story of Andhra Pradesh, although also actively promoting foreign investment, seems to have a key feature in the need to involve the Chief Minister in every major deal. The full implications of this have, as of yet, not been fully understood. But it seems clear that the personal ambitions of the leaders of the state go a long way towards understanding who is awarded contracts for mines whether they are foreign or Indian.[6] One scandal concerned the son of the former Chief Minister and his investment in Raghuram Cements which came with a mining lease for limestone. Another major 'investor' in AP has been the former Karnataka BJP Tourism Minister from Bellary, Gali Janardhan Reddy, who via his new and completely unknown company, Brahmani Steels, managed to get the mining lease for the Obulapuram iron ore mines in Anantapur district.

Given the lack of information about mining in tribal areas, this report focuses on large-scale mining such as bauxite and coal for which at least some information is available. Much of minor mineral mining remain unknown and largely unregulated, whether it occurs in the Scheduled or non-Scheduled areas of the state and require further research.

In Andhra Pradesh, like in other tribal-dominated areas, people have had to fight for their rights to land and resources for centuries. During the British colonial rule, the frequent

---

6. In the period 2004-2009, the CM's son went from being unknown to becoming a significant investor in media (Sakshi), cement (Raghuram Cements), IT and many other forms of business in Andhra Pradesh. At no point has it been made clear where the money to invest came from.

rebellions became such an obstacle to the colonial power's need for order that the rebellious areas were set aside from the normal rule of law. Thus were created the special areas in which the Agent of the government ruled according to a different set of laws compared to the rest of British India. This happened in coastal Andhra Pradesh, then a part of the Madras Presidency, with the creation of the 'Vizagapatam and Ganjam Agency Areas Act of 1833'. Similar regulations were brought into Hyderabad state. These 'agency areas' had their borders shifted over the years but have remained more or less the same since the late 19th century. Since independence they have become part of the Scheduled Areas with constitutional protection as well as state legal protection.

One of the most difficult issues in the Scheduled Areas has been over the control of forests. The forest settlement, which placed most available land in the hands of the government, increased the number of rebellions. After significant controversy, recognition of the need to protect tribal rights to agricultural land was extended without including the issue of forest.[7] After further unrest, land rights legislation was additionally strengthened via amendments, the most recent of these occurred in Srikakulam district in 1969. Rights to forest land are only being acknowledged in recent years via the Forest Rights Act of 2006. Since this act is yet to be fully implemented it is not further discussed here.

The main protection for tribal land is thus the Andhra Pradesh Scheduled Areas Land Transfer Regulation (APSLTR) 1959, amended last in 1970 (therefore known as the 1/70 Act). This land transfer act is of special importance in Andhra Pradesh since it bans transfer of any land to a non-tribal person, whether officially owned by a tribal farmer or by the government itself. This is different compared to, for example, the Odisha equivalent Land Transfer Act, which

---

7. The first law to protect tribal land against alienation was the Agency Tracts Interest and Land Transfer Act 1917 (Madras Act 1 of 1917).

is only concerned with the land officially owned by tribal farmers, leaving the majority of land as government-owned land which can be transferred to private industry.

The ban on selling or leasing land was affirmed in Andhra Pradesh, specifically for private mineral industry, in the 1997 Supreme Court 'Samatha Judgement'. A major drawback in the judgement was however that the government or public sector industry was allowed to carry on its operations as before, including the large Singareni Colleries coal mines.[8] Responses to the judgement from successive governments in the state as well as at the Centre have unfortunately been to attempt to amend or circumvent it rather than taking it as a call to actually include the people immediately affected when making plans of how various resources in the area should be used and for whose benefit.[9] The Samatha Judgement has come to be seen by governments and courts as limited to only Andhra Pradesh though no final judgement exists to confirm this. Rather than attempting to expand the scope of the Samatha Judgement to other mining-affected communities across the states with Scheduled Area, efforts are currently on to circumvent the Judgement also in Andhra Pradesh by using an empty public sector company as a facade to allow private mining (see Bauxite chapter below).

---

8. Supreme Court of India, 1997.
9. See, for example, the attempt to have the judgement overruled in the Supreme Court of India (2000), or the attempt to circumvent it by the Ministry of Mines, 2000.

2

Coal

Officially coal mining is still reserved for the public sector but a large loophole has been opened up for what is called 'captive mining', essentially a private company mining coal for its own needs, which can be to power a steel plant, aluminium smelter or simply to produce power. Another form of privatisation is the increasing use of contractors to excavate coal on behalf of Coal India. Using a contractor is a common feature also in private mining, making the monitoring and accountability of companies towards working conditions as well as environmental mitigation more difficult. The 11th Five Year Plan requires captive mining to grow by 35-40% in order to meet its projections.[10]

Coal mining remains regulated by the Ministry of Coal as opposed to other large-scale mining which is under the Ministry of Mines. With electricity demand growing exponentially in India, much focus in policy circles has centred around how to fill the 30 million ton gap per year between demand and the production of Coal India's various coalfields. Government plans do not see the amount of coal available as a significant problem:

> Coal-resources are not in short supply. The major hurdles to the multi-pronged effort needed to increase production are the procedural roadblocks in activating the requisite number of

10. Ministry of Mines, 2009.

> coalmines, which can yield production in the quickest possible time.[11]

In 2000, only 10% of all coal was imported and then mainly of special grades not available in India for steel plants. A new development is the extensive plans for thermal power plants along the coast of Andhra Pradesh feeding on imported coal, presumed to come mainly from Indonesia.[12] One reading of this could be that India, like the United States, Europe and China earlier, has now become an importer of socially and environmentally difficult mining from even poorer countries. A different reason could be lowered import custom duties which are only now making it viable to import coal. Since most coal is anyhow transported long distances from the mines of central tribal India to the users in the metropolitan areas of the north, west and south of the country, transportation by ship, even from other countries, might not be very much more expensive than domestic train transport. Whatever the case may be, import of coal is expected to be another major source for power generation in the coming years.

Indian coal is generally high in ash content and low in calorific content.[13] For these reasons, this coal is only likely to be used for domestic power production (accounting for 67%). The steel industry remains a big customer though the coal needs intense washing to be useful for the industry (13% of total use), but much coking coal is imported.[14] Cement production is another big user of coal which coincides with the existing large-scale limestone mining in Andhra Pradesh.

11. Ministry of Coal, 2005:2.
12. See, for example, the multiple power plants of up to 12,000 MW planned as part of the VANPIC project, or the Sompetha Thermal power plant in coastal Andhra Pradesh.
13. A low calorific content means each ton of coal will produce less energy than compared to coal with a higher value.
14. International Energy Agency, 2002.

2.1 Coal in Andhra Pradesh

Coal in Andhra Pradesh exists in the Godavari River valley with 8% of India's total coal deposits. The deposit stretches for more than 350 kms along the river in the districts of Warangal, Adilabad, Karimnagar, Khammam and West Godavari. The Singareni Colleries are currently attempting to strongly increase its mining via open cast mining. Open cast coal mining is at present responsible for more than 75% of Singareni's coal production while only employing 15% of the workers (Singareni Colleries 2010). Between 1997 and 2002, almost all open cast mines were economically profitable for Singareni while the opposite was true for the underground mines (Comptroller and Auditor General of India 2002). The mines which are the most expensive for local livelihoods and the environment are thus the most profitable for Singareni Colleries.

Singareni started open cast mining in the late 1970s having earlier relied entirely on underground mining. Nowadays the company is intent on using only open cast methods for its new mines since "[o]pencast mining ensures a quick build-up of production, large quantum of production and maximum possible recovery of coal (Singareni Colleries 2011)." But not only will all new mines be open cast, existing underground mines will, wherever possible, be converted to open cast. In an MoEF expert committee meeting, the Director of Singareni in 2009 stated that "[t]he present plan is to open all [underground] mines to extract the residual coal ..." (Ministry of Environment and Forests, 2009). The expansion of open cast coal mining and the subsequent loss of jobs and increased environmental problems are not unique to Singareni Colleries. It has been widely talked about within Coal India for many years (Lahiri-Dutt, 1999). The power generation crisis, with increased emphasis on increased open cast coal mining, has meant additional changes in the recent decade.

Despite the frequent private mining in other states of the country, and the AP government's active support for private investment in other parts of the economy, coal mining continues to be done almost only by Singareni Collieries in the state. The table below summarises exploration activities by other companies other than Singareni Collieries. As can be seen, none of the companies are private as is the case in many other parts of India.

Table 1: Captive Mining in Andhra Pradesh

Name of Mining Company	*Date of Allotment*	*Name of Coal Block*	*Coalfield*	*Status*
Andhra Pradesh Power Generation Corporation	December 6, 2005	Tadicherla-I	Singareni Collieries	Exploration
Andhra Pradesh Power Generation Corporation	February 20, 2007	Anesttipali	Singareni Collieries	Exploration
Andhra Pradesh Power Generation Corporation	February 20, 2007	Punkula-Chilka	Godavari Valley (assumed to be Singareni Collieries)	Exploration
Andhra Pradesh Power Generation Corporation	May 29, 2007	Penagada-par	Singareni Collieries	Exploration
Unallocated		Cherla Open Cast	Singareni Collieries	
Unallocated		Cherla Underground	Singareni	Collieries
Unallocated		Tadicherla block II	Singareni Collieries	
Andhra Pradesh Mineral Development (APMDC)	August 2, 2006	Nuagaon Telisahi, Orissa	Talcher	Exploration

Source: Meeting minutes June 22-23, 2009 reviewing captive coal leases, Ministry of Coal.

2.2 About the Singareni Collieries

Coal in Andhra Pradesh exists in the Godavari valley with 8% of India's total coal deposits.[15] The deposit stretches for more than 350 kms along the Godavari River in the districts of Warangal, Adilabad, Karimnagar, Khammam and West Godavari. It is estimated that the deposits contain 9 billion tons of coal which are expected to last for more than a century. A significant section of these deposits fall under the Fifth Schedule Area (See Annexure 1 for the list of Scheduled Areas of the state), but since public sector Singareni Collieries has operated there since pre-independence times, it has never been questioned whether they have the right to do so or not. Public sector entities have the right to operate in the AP Scheduled Areas according to the Samatha Judgement. Coal mining continues without the consent of the local population and without any particular provisions for local benefit-sharing.

The separate entity of Singareni Collieries compared to the rest of Coal India is due to its history as a separately incorporated coal mining company in 1889. At one point, the company was even stock-listed in London. In 1945, it was purchased by the then Hyderabad State to become India's first public sector coal mining company. Since 1949, the Singareni Collieries operates under an Industrial Trust Fund with the controlling interest being with the AP government, but a minority share is held by the central government via Coal India Ltd. More than 80% of the company's coal production is being supplied to thermal power plants with the rest going to cement and other coal-based industries.

Approximately half of this coal is from 0-300 metres above ground, an almost similar amount is from 300-600 metres below the surface and a sixth is from below this depth reaching as deep as 1200 metres. Eight hundred and seventy-

15. The same deposit continues further north into other major coal mining areas such as Maharashtra's Chandra-Wardha region and further into Madhya Pradesh and Tawa valley.

eight million tons of coal have been mined till date from the various mines of the collieries.

The older coal mines at Singareni were underground, but as it has been found to be too expensive, underground mines are on average twice as expensive compared to open cast, a move has been made towards open cast in recent years in line with the general trend in India. Since many of the social and environmental costs are not included in the cost of the more damaging open cast mines, these are bound to come out as more efficient than the underground mines. Nevertheless, the shift away from underground operations is not a complete one as can be seen in the tables below. Efforts are also on to make the underground mining more efficient in terms of output through, for example, the Kakatiya longwall project.

The collieries are currently attempting to strongly increase its mining. The Annexure 2 lists current plans for 7 new open cast mines and 12 underground mines. For these new mines, as well as for the renewal of old mines, 5,059 hectares of forest are currently pending clearance with various regulatory authorities. The company is also waiting for 10,023 hectares of mining lease area similarly pending approval with the Ministry of Mines. Singareni Collieries has also decided to establish power plants powered from its coal mines. A 2*300 MW thermal power plant at Jaipur village in Adilabad received environmental clearance in October 2009. This will be powered by coal from Srirampur coal mines 8.8 kms away and use water from the Chevella project on the Godavari River. For the 308 ha required for the power plant, it was stated that no R&R is involved though no explanation was given in the approval as to why this land was empty of residents.[16]

---

16. Government of India, Ministry of Environment and Forests. *Environmental Clearance Letter to Singareni Colleries*, October 29, 2009.

2.3 Environment and Livelihoods Impact

The main difference between coal mining and other forms of mining is the enormous size of its operations. Even major metals like iron or bauxite will usually not be mined to a similar size, especially not in any one location. Coal expands over vast territories and thus risks affecting more people than any other form of mining. This is particularly true for open cast mining which has become even more common in recent years as higher output has been sought. One positive benefit of coal mining is however its lower toxicity compared to many metals where the overburden and the open mines themselves may leach metals into the groundwater for many years.

Common complaints over coal mining include:

- Displacement (especially for open cast mines)
- Deforestation (especially for open cast mines)
- Loss of groundwater (especially for open cast mines)
- Workplace accidents (especially for underground mines)
- Underground fires

In underground mining, a shaft is drilled into the mountain until the ore body is reached. Open cast mining means removing significant amounts of soil and other minerals till the ore body is uncovered and can be mined. The removed material is referred to as the overburden and is usually much larger than the amount mined. Singareni coal mines have as much as 6 times the amount of overburden compared to the amount of coal mined. This is known as 1:6 strip ratio. In 2005-06, Singareni Collieries generated 115 million tons of overburden which it had to dispose of in order to reach the coal. More than half of this disposal was managed by outsourced private contractors.

Some of the main differences between the two types of coal mining will then be that underground mining, at least theoretically, can keep most of the land use above ground as it was prior to commencement of mining whether used for agriculture or is a forest. Open cast mining will irrevocably mean that no other activity can take place as long as mining goes on. Labour safety has been a particular issue with underground mines since the walls and roofs are prone to collapsing unless great caution is exercised.

Table 2: Comparing Open Cast and Underground Coal Mining

Open Cast Operations	Underground Operations
– 13 Mines – 25.8 million tonnes – Overburden of 140 million cubic metres (2006-07) – Stripping Ratio: up to 1:6 – Depths Operated: 170 m – Depths Planned: 400 m	– Operational Profile – 42 Mines – Coal: 11.9 million tonnes (2006-07) – Depths Operated: 400 m – Depths Planned: 650 m
Open Cast Technology	**Underground Technology**
– Surface Miner – Dragline – Shovel & Dumper – Inpit Crusher – Conveyer – Spreader – Highwall	– Side Discharge Loader – Load Haul Dumper – Road Header – Longwall – Blasting Gallery – Continuous Miner

Open cast mines leave 'footprints' clearly visible even from satellite photography like those available on Google Earth. Groundwater would be expected to be high in the vicinity of the river meaning that special care would have to be taken to avoid water from seeping into the mine. Immediately west of the open cast mine is the location for the proposed Kondagudem underground mine. Underground mines can sometimes also be seen from satellite photos like the Bhupalpalli mine. A closer inspection would have to be done to determine the local effects of the underground mine, but at least the visible impact is much smaller.

2.3.1 Coal Mining and the Environment

Both underground and open cast mines come with the risk of interfering with groundwater, putting the workers at risk in the case of underground mines, and threatening the flow and availability of water in surrounding areas in the case of open cast mines. Because of its tendency to drain water into the mining pit, open cast mines tend to be high energy users since water has to be continuously pumped out to allow for mining. Once drained out of the mining pit, the water will be made to drain away from the actual area causing a depleting groundwater table unless special care is taken. The EIA for the proposed Kondapuram underground coal mine deals only very briefly with potential water problems asserting that "[t]here will not be any significant impact on water environment due to the proposed underground coal mining operations. The mine discharge water and workshop effluents will be treated before using it for different activities at the mine."[17]

Open cast mining inevitably means a loss of forest and other vegetation which once existed on the surface. Given the vast size of coal mines, large areas of forest have been lost in the past. While mining of major minerals has been made to include an afforestation plan in all mining plans since 2002 by the Ministry of Mines, the same has not happened for coal mining leaving much of the actual forest plantations ad hoc depending on the interests of the particular mining company.[18] Singareni Collieries currently has 5,059 hectares of land pending for forest clearance (See Table 2 of Annexure 1).

The Supreme Court has intervened in the procedure for forest land diversion and made compensatory afforestation mandatory for all mining activities including the payment of a net present value for the existing forest. While huge sums of money have been transferred to the account of the MoEF in Delhi, it has not been known how it should be spent. When details do emerge, examples like the case of a Singareni coal mine in Khammam district provides a terrible example of

17. Singareni Colleries, 2008:7.
18. Bhushan & Zeya, 2008.

afforestation causing double displacement. Once forest land had been diverted for a coal mine in Khammam district, new land is needed to be acquired for afforestation. Ten thousand hectares of land were identified in West Godavari district for plantation of the new forest causing the local Konda Reddy tribals to protest.[19]

Another issue with compensatory afforestation is that when the new forest is being planted, there are no efforts to involve people, either displaced from the coal mine or from the afforestation land. The legislation on forest compensation is still evolving but for now the new forest seems to be commercial forest plantations which will only serve narrow company interests rather than attempt to re-create the livelihoods and environments which were upset by the mining. This is how Singareni describes its work to restore mined out areas: "The company has taken a major initiative to green all areas. In the areas where precious topsoil is being lost due to activities like brick kiln making etc., had been brought under green cover. In these areas industrial plantations have been raised to meet the timber needs for underground mines besides reaping the incidental environmental benefits."[20] About 1,230,680 seedlings were planted covering an area of 713 hectares in 2004-5 by the company.[21]

In the meantime, the implementation of the Forest Rights Act is ongoing while at the same time coal mining and its afforestation activities are permanently removing land which most likely would have been claimed as the right of tribal people. Major extents of land can be expected to be diverted in the future for coal mining. The Coal Vision 2025 of the Government of India states that the requirement of forest land for mining would increase more than threefold from the current 22,000 ha to 73, 000 ha.[22]

---

19. Sarin, 2009.
20. Singareni Colleries, 2006: 14.
21. Singareni Colleries, 2005.
22. Ministry of Coal, 2005.

2.3.2 *Displacement from Mines*

As is discussed further in the section on bauxite mining, displacement due to mining but also from the afforestation areas is a serious issue. Despite the ongoing agitation for decades against displacement, minimal progress has been made in Andhra Pradesh. In some cases it even seems like earlier progress towards better compensation has been reversed after it was shown to be difficult to give land for land compensation. In coal mining, increased production to bridge the existing power generation shortages are often deemed more important than the issues of the displaced. Even proper information on the number of displaced is difficult to come by, but it seems clear that only a fraction of the population displaced was ever attempted to be rehabilitated.

It is well known that displacement affects tribals and Dalits disproportionally to other people. This is partially due to the areas where especially tribals live coincide with the existence of minerals which can be mined, rivers which can be dammed, and forests which can be used for paper industry and other purposes. Up to 80% of all people displaced from coal mines and 60% of the displaced from other forms of mining have been Adivasis across India.[23] Coal Vision 2025 estimate that 170,000 families or 850,000 displaced persons would have to be rehabilitated by 2025 when the requirement for land would double from the current 147,000 ha to 292,500 ha and a significant number of these could be expected to be in Andhra Pradesh.

The lack of access to formal education and the economic vulnerability of tribal people have also tended to make them easier to displace since they are less likely to be able to demand proper compensation compared to other groups. This sad state of affairs continues to this very day. One important reason is that tribal ownership of land was never recognised even during colonial times. When a coal mine is

23. Fernandes, 2009.

established today, the official records are likely to say that all the land is forest and that the land acquisition is a matter of diverting forest land from the forest department to the mining company, including compensation for afforestation activities.

The AP R&R policy 2005 requires all acquired land from a tribal person to lead to mandatory land for land compensation and is, in this sense, more generous than most rehabilitation policies across the country today. But unfortunately, there is only a very small portion of all land holdings which has ever been recognised, legally making most tribals officially encroachers. The land most likely to be mined for coal as well as other minerals will be hilly terrain which is likely to be notified as forest land, while a small number of people having private *pattas* will have their land on flat valley land away from any potential mining site. Fernandes mentions that 32% of all land in AP acquired in tribal as well as non-tribal areas from 1951-1995 was common property land including forest (out of a total 1 million hectares acquired).[24]

A few examples can be used to examine how coal mines in Andhra Pradesh are planned and what information is provided about them. Kondapur mine is an underground mine proposed on an area of 473 hectares in Manuguru Mandal of Khammam district. This location is about 15 kms north of Badrachalam in an area which is entirely a part of the Scheduled Area. This aspect is not mentioned by the EIA since it does not affect the company's operations as a public sector entity. Similarly, there is no mention about the location of Jalagam Vengala Rao open cast-II (JVR-II) coal mining project in Sattupally Mandal, a partially declared Scheduled Area.[25]

---

24. Fernandes, 2009.
25. Singareni Colleries, 2009. This new mine is a continuation of the Sattupalli Block-I (JVR OC-I Expansion Project) which is currently operating immediately to the north of the proposed site.

Despite being underground, the Kondapur coal mine will need to acquire 150 hectares of land owing to the risk of subsidence that is the risk of the mine caving in. The EIA declares this land to be fully forest land and thus there will be no need for any rehabilitation. Within a 10 km radius of the project site 11,116 people live, but how many of them live in the forest area proposed for mining is not revealed. The benefit to local people, who may or may not be displaced, is "indirect employment opportunities [...] in contractual works like construction of infrastructural facilities, transportation, sanitation, for supply of goods and services to the mine and other community services."[26] Direct employment is reserved for workers already employed elsewhere by the company leading to the conclusion that the new mine will not lead to any new employment opportunities. Similarly for the JVR-II mine, "most of the manpower for this project will be adjusted from other mines after providing necessary training."[27]

The JVR-II mine being open cast, will need 1,410 hectares of land out of which 788.22 hectares are described as forest land and the remaining 621.59 hectares as non-forest land. "The number of Project Displaced Families (PDFs) in Kommepalli, village is 120 and the number of Project Affected Families (PAFs) in Kommepalli, Kistaram, Errakunta and Rejerla villages are 392, 77, 6 and 96 respectively."[28] This means a total of 691 families are considered as displaced or affected and will be rehabilitated giving a tacit acknowledgement that the area is indeed Scheduled since it is only in the Scheduled Areas where all loss of land leads to mandatory rehabilitation according to the rehabilitation policy of Andhra Pradesh.[29]

---

26. Singareni Colleries, 2008:10.
27. Singareni Colleries, 2009:5.
28. Singareni Colleries, 2009:15.
29. Singareni Colleries, 2009 and Government of Andhra Pradesh, 2005 & 2006.

For the displaced who cannot even hope for a job in the mines, the EIAs state the following: "The proposed mine is likely to have a positive impact on the socio-economic status of the people in the region. In more than 100 years of coal mining in SCCL mining areas, no significant changes have been observed in the traditional way of life and occupation of the local people in coal mining areas."[30] Clearly some independent work is needed to evaluate what has actually happened in the coal mining areas.

2.4 Workers at the Coal Mines

Singareni Colleries is a company under strong pressure to become profitable and more productive in addition to the perceived need for it to expand its mining. In 2004-05, it was reported that 91,970 people worked for the company which was already a radical reduction from 2000-01 when 105,627 people were employed. Consequently the productivity went up from 1.25 to 1.62 tons of coal per employee.[31] In 2005-06, the number of employees was down to 86,025 followed by 69,540 as of November 30, 2009.[32] It is not clear how many workers the company expects to have in the future, but it seems unlikely that more people will be employed given the increased mechanisation. Consequently, with the pressure to reduce staff, the number of strikes has declined radically. The lowest number of strikes was recorded since 1976-77, during the Emergency years, was in 2004-05.

Prospects for work for tribal people must remain limited given the reductions in overall staff. There is no mention of jobs for the local Adivasis or training to allow them to become eligible in government reports, such as the annual report of the human resources department for 2007-08. Presumably, some tribal people must have jobs within the corporation

30. Singareni Colleries, 2008:9.
31. Singareni Colleries, 2005.
32. Singareni Colleries website, http://scclmines.com/home.asp [Accessed December 30, 2009]
33. Singareni Colleries, 2004 & 2005.

but if this is the case, no statistics are presented in the examined annual reports.[33] Where rehabilitation policies for other types of mines often promise a job per displaced family, the Singareni Colleries promises no such thing.

Underground mines have, in the past, been very labour-intensive which created several jobs but the working conditions have often been extremely dangerous when tunnels cave in over workers. It is also common for methane within the coal to explode and cause serious accidents in underground coal mines. 40% of all accidents in Indian mines up to 1995 accounting for the lives of 839 workers were found to have involved methane. The 22 underground mines of Singareni Colleries had 25,000 people employed and could not be mechanised due to old age and low production. Still they remained operating since 12% of the total output came from these mines.[34] The trend on safety seems to be improving according to official statistics. Seven people suffered fatal accidents in 2005-06. Further, there were 15 fatalities in 2004-05 and 45 in 2003-04.[35] A reverse trend is visible in serious injuries, according to statistics the company has started to record recently, these increased from 294 in 2004-05 to 804 in 2005-06.

2.5 Case Study: Coal Mining in Manuguru of Khammam District

This case study builds on the results of a livelihoods study (Oskarsson, 2011), with fieldwork in April and August 2011 at two expanding coal mines in Manuguru of Khammam District. The first of these is the so-called Manuguru Open Cast II Expansion, an already existing major open cast mine now scheduled to become even larger to eventually use 3,200 hectares of land in total, and the second is the Manuguru Open Cast, a new mine planned on top of an old, exhausted underground mine on 486 hectares of largely fertile double

34. Singareni Colleries, 2006.
35. Singareni Colleries, 2005.

crop land. The first mine will officially displace three villages with 330 households, while the latter will displace four villages with 1,248 households. The two mines have received all administrative clearances, including those by MoEF, but land acquisition issues have stalled implementation of the Manuguru open cast mine. They are within a few kilometres from one another indicating a need to investigate the overall impact of several mines in the local area (Environmental Protection Training and Research Institute 2007; Ministry of Environment and Forests, 2008b; Ministry of Environment and Forests, 2008a).

Manuguru is a significant area of coal mining. It is however not necessarily unique, either as a coal producing area, or due to its operations being in a sensitive Scheduled Area. Similar large-scale open cast mining is currently operating in a number of other locations in the region by the same mining company and in close proximity to poor farmers, many of whom are Scheduled Tribes. Manuguru, despite being one of the more remote towns in Khammam District close to the Chhattisgarh border, is not necessarily unique either in the large influx of non-tribal peoples in recent decades, or in the way that coal mining and related industries have changed the local economy. Towns within the District like Palvoncha, Yllendu and Kothagudem, the latter being the corporate headquarters of Singareni Colleries, are all rapidly growing smaller urban centres with significant coal economies. Agriculture continues to be the main source of livelihood in Khammam District however. In many cases, agricultural land is still officially owned by tribes while the users and main beneficiaries are non-tribal farmers. The high incidence of farmland held by non-tribals, especially in the Telangana Scheduled Areas, is well-known with more than 50% of all land held by non-tribal farmers (Rao et al., 2006).

So how does underground compare to open cast mining? By opencasting a mine the excavation of coal starts from ground-level and works downwards. In the process, it is only natural that no other activities can take place on the same land unlike underground mining where, apart from a few entry and exit points, land use on top can usually remain unchanged. Since the amount of overburden (OB) excavated from open cast mining is many times larger than the amount of coal, at Manuguru where it is about seven times in volume (Environmental Protection Training and Research Institute 2007), additional land becomes necessary for storing this waste. This land can be as much as half the size of the entire mine. The reason for this can be seen for a mine like the Manuguru OC II Expansion which is planned to be 400 metres deep while the overburden dump is restricted to a height of 120 metres by the MoEF thereby requiring a larger area for storage. Once the coal has been exhausted some, though far from all, of the overburden is shifted back into the empty coal pit. At closure a 90 m deep pit (in the case of the Manuguru OC II Expansion mine) and some of the overburden hills remain as permanent reminders of the open cast coal mining creating difficulties in ever returning the land to cultivation (Ibid.).

A natural consequence of the open cast expansion is thus the increased use of land. Environmental clearance documents from the Ministry of Environment and Forests mention a total amount of land of 16,114 ha of land having been approved, or being about to be approved, for open cast mining by Singareni for the years 2007-10. Of this land, 5,988 ha was officially classified as agricultural land and 5,839 ha was forest. Many other types of land were also included, close to 2,000 ha of government land and waste land, both of which, like the categories of forest and private land, are likely to contain significant areas used in support of rural livelihoods (Oskarsson, 2011). This recent expansion is naturally in addition to the historical land use of Singareni. Between 1995 and 2005, 8,644 ha of forest land was diverted in Andhra Pradesh for coal mining by the company according to the MoEF (Ministry of Environment and Forests, 2005).

Singareni admits that there are limits to how much open cast mining can be carried out based on economic and environmental grounds: "The constraint to the application of open cast mining is the economic limits of stripping ratio and to some extent the damage to the surface environment (Singareni Colleries, 2011)." Delays and cancellations are common for many of the open cast mines. Twenty-two of the 34 projects currently under implementation are either delayed or on hold according to the Ministry of Coal (Ministry of Coal, 2011). Production has nevertheless been increasing to reach 38 million tons in 2010. This is well behind the production target of 46 million for Singareni, but nevertheless closer to target than other public coal companies which only managed between 51% and 65% of target (Ministry of Coal, 2011).

Open cast operations allow larger machinery and bigger blasting operations to take place thus reducing the need for workers. Consequently the number of workers has been reduced dramatically despite the increased production. Singareni had 68,000 employees in 2010, down from 1.12 lakh employees in 1998 (Comptroller and Auditor General of India 2002; Ministry of Coal 2011). With this reduction in the number of workers, Singareni has not been able to offer any jobs to the displaced for several decades now (Oskarsson, 2011). One benefit of open cast mining, apart from increased production, has however been the improvement of worker safety.

2.5.1 *Livelihoods Outcomes at Manuguru*

The livelihood implications of open cast coal mining in Manuguru were analysed according to a) the mine establishment which displaces farmers, herders and many others, b) the operating mine which creates a number of environmental costs but also offers the main potential benefit in terms of jobs, and c) mine closure in which the land potentially could be returned to the original landlosers, or at the very least be shaped for new livelihood uses, but in reality appears to be handed over to the forest department without community consultations.

The land losers from the two mines of Manuguru were found to be a very varied set of people consisting of tribes, Dalits and a wide range of mainly BC (OBC) groups. Due to many decades of migration from other parts of Andhra Pradesh, both as a result of agricultural land grab in this nominally tribal area and the availability of well-paying jobs at Singareni, the tribes were found to be in a clear minority even in the forest areas. Their low educational qualifications and subordinated social position meant that they have lost large tracts of agricultural land to outside farmers and miners. Though there are a few organisations working on behalf of the tribes, the people still to date have to rely on government benevolence to implement the greater legal benefits they have compared to other people in the AP R&R Bill (Government of Andhra Pradesh 2005; Government of Andhra Pradesh, Irrigation and CAD Department 2006), whereas other groups in Manuguru have a better ability to demand rights themselves. In the Manuguru case, one displaced tribal village had indeed been resettled in 1998 and provided new land, though poor in quality and far from the new resettled village.

The Manuguru OC II Expansion mine operates in a forest area inhabited by tribal and Dalit groups, but with few actual land titles, resulting in low chances for anything other than cash compensation for the houses of the displaced. This was where the above mentioned tribal villages have been resettled with new, smaller-sized agricultural land and a lack of forest access which had earlier supplemented farm income. This form of resettlement, however incomplete, was nevertheless much better than the cash only compensation offered to neighbouring non-tribal villages affected by the same mine. The second mine studied, the Manuguru OC, was planned on fertile agricultural land, mainly inhabited by non-tribal groups. The significant displacement, where it appeared as if the project planners preferred to acquire agricultural land to nearby degraded forest, and the high quality of land had generated strong opposition delaying the mine for several years. At the time of fieldwork, some land had been acquired, but no further work was visible on the ground.

The mainly non-tribal farmers without land titles, agricultural labourers and those who survive on common property resources such as forest produce collection and grazing land receive little or no compensation when coal mining expands. Similarly, those who do not immediately lose their land but live close enough to lose access to water, or have to face blasts and dust, are also distinctly worse off from the mining. Any issue which falls outside of the direct displacement remains not compensated for. In Manuguru, this particularly related to damaged houses due to mine explosions and the reduced availability of groundwater in some of the villages close to the Manuguru OC II Expansion mine.

During the active coal mining phase, it was found that the large-scale expansion in coal production resulted in no new jobs, even for those who were qualified to apply, due to mechanisation and existing surplus staff at other locations of Singareni Colleries. Singareni, to some extent, attempted to provide training for other professions, but otherwise the only jobs available were those coming from private contractors who manage the overburden, transport of coal and many other tasks related to mining. The exact number of such jobs is not known; only a handful of the respondents met during fieldwork had been able to secure jobs like security guards or truck drivers. For most people, mining was something they had to learn to live with and adjust to while attempting to continue already existing agricultural livelihoods as best as possible.

Once the coal has been mined out, what remains is an only partially refilled crater since it is seen as too expensive to completely restore the land to its pre-mining condition. Eventually the mined out crater is expected to accumulate rain water and potentially become a lake. Surrounding the lake will be large overburden hills of 90-120 metres height. The entire mined out land is turned over to the Forest

Department without any involvement of those who earlier lost their land to the mine. How the lake and its water are to be managed remains unknown since it is not mentioned in available planning documents. Neither Panchayats nor the Forest Rights Act are taken into account in the afforestation activities leaving great uncertainty for the long-term future of livelihoods in Manuguru, when returning the land to the communities could have ensured long-term equity in the area.

The central narrative which emerges is of denied community involvement in planning, operating and closing the open cast coal mines of Manuguru. This lack of community concerns makes it appear as if these mines are indeed jobless openings which serve to further impoverish an already marginalised and vulnerable local population with only very few exceptions. Given the strength of local tribal rights movements, as well as the ongoing Telangana agitation, open cast coal mining, or simply OC, might therefore become the next major resource struggle in the area unless social concerns are better taken into account. This region has seen its resources being extracted by outsiders for generations, but is not likely to remain silent in the future.

2.6 Conclusion

Coal mining is a major activity across four districts in the Adivasi areas of Andhra Pradesh. Unfortunately, there is precious little information about even basic aspects of the mines and their impact like the extent of operations, number of people displaced and related environmental issues. Since the company is a public sector entity, it can operate freely in the area without contravening the AP Land Transfer regulation or the Samatha Judgement. The poverty and remoteness of the areas have ensured that limited civil society pressure has been possible to build up at all to make the issues of coal mining become apparent. Affected people have been kept out of the process of land acquisition since most of the land has been settled as forest land. Additionally, security concerns tend to catch local people in the middle of skirmishes between police and Naxalites creating difficult conditions for public protest.

Coal mining occurs exclusively away from the attention of urban India and has not caught the attention it deserves. The use of major areas of land and the increasing open cast operations will be unrivalled to any other form of mining in India in terms of sheer land degradation. Much work needs to be done to understand where and when coal mines operate in relation to Scheduled Area land, including how these mines affect Adivasis and the environments they live in. The Manuguru case study presented here can serve as one instance to highlight the impact of coal.

Where mining takes place, it would be much needed to see studies on the mitigation efforts which take place, and how these could be made more participatory and sensitive to local needs. Compared to industrial or real estate land, a mine will only operate for at most a couple of decades and there is at least, theoretically, a possibility to return the land to the original owners/users. At present plans seem to be to create forest plantations for commercial use rather than return them to local people for the benefit of livelihoods. Extensive work is needed to change this approach towards a more pro-poor orientation.

3

Bauxite[36]

More than 30 years since first discovered, the major bauxite deposits of the Visakhapatnam Adivasi areas continue to cause controversy. Since the elections in 2004, it is the Congress government which is promoting these projects, where the earlier TDP government failed, by signing two MoUs and planning for even more. The most recent attempts to implement bauxite projects started on July 1, 2005 when an MoU between Jindal South West (JSW) of the Jindal Group and the government of Andhra Pradesh was signed. This was followed by a second MoU one and a half years later on February 14, 2007 between RAK, an enterprise of the Government of Ras al-Khaima from the United Arab Emirates, and the AP Government. The two cases were identical in its plans to mine bauxite from the agency areas of Visakhapatnam district via government-owned APMDC (Andhra Pradesh Mineral Development Corporation), sell this at a discount rate to an alumina refinery established by the private industry, and in a later phase smelt the alumina into aluminium.

Congress Party resistance to bauxite while in opposition changed within less than one year of coming to power, while

36. This section on bauxite is an updated version of an article originally written for the bulletin of the Human Rights Forum, published in June 2009.

the TDP in opposition has made amazing discoveries of all the ills these projects will befall on 'the people'. A high point in the lows of populist politics was reached when Chandrababu Naidu was travelling on a bullock cart through the areas to be acquired for the ANRAK aluminium complex in Makavaripalem of Visakhapatnam district.[37] This is the same Chandrababu who in power used every trick in the book to attempt amendments to both AP laws governing land rights for tribal people as well as the constitutional protection of Scheduled Areas, to be able to establish bauxite mining and alumina refining in cooperation with a Dubai investor. The civil society opposition which prevented plans during the Naidu regime seems to be failing at present with the new government having worked out ways to overcome the earlier issues while also showing greater determination to implement the projects.

Bauxite was first discovered in the mid-1970s in Andhra Pradesh and Odisha but since the deposits in Odisha are larger, the first industries were located there with the establishment of Nalco in Damanjodi in the mid-1980s. Similar industry and mines were attempted to be set up in AP with Russian collaboration, but stalled due to a lack of foreign currency, control of technology and energy problems. These were finally abandoned with the fall of the Soviet Union in 1991. It is only since the mid to late 1990s as money and technology became available that civil society awakening to the negative consequences of bauxite mining started to play a factor in delaying the projects.

This chapter details how the AP Government and its partners in industry have been working to implement the bauxite projects. Further it discusses how the valid concerns raised over what will happen to tribal lands and livelihoods, water availability along the already water-deficient coast, and

37. *The Hindu*. People accord rousing reception to Naidu, 21 Dec 2007. http://www.hindu.com/2007/12/21/stories/2007122154840600.htm

environmental problems from bauxite mining industry have been side-lined. When the economic benefits locally as well as for the state are shown to be modest, questions are raised as to whom actually the benefits go from the proposed projects.

3.1 Project Planning

The basic plan, which is being repeated in the two current projects, have the following components:

1. An MoU is signed between the company and the state government to formalise the business agreement.
2. APMDC applies for mining leases, environmental clearances and forest clearances for the proposed mines spread across the Scheduled Areas of Visakhapatnam district. According to the MoUs signed, the costs are actually paid by the private industry. Even the cost of compensatory afforestation estimated at Rs. 80 crores for the Jindal project alone is borne by the company.
3. EIA applications for mine and refinery are dealt with separately as has become standard practice in similar projects across India. Once the clearance is given for the refinery, this major investment can be used to as leverage towards a clearance for the mines.[38] Additionally in this case, the government wants to ensure that the private investment is coming to the state, which means it will require the refinery to be approved before the mine.
4. The alumina refinery will be located outside the Scheduled Areas to avoid tribal land transfer regulations but inside the state limits of Andhra Pradesh to allow more money to be invested in the state. Again, all expenses are paid by the company,

38. A refinery will cost several thousand crore rupees while a bauxite mine is a relatively low cost operation.

but with intense government intervention administratively to acquire the land, and politically to suppress local farmer opposition.

5. Aluminium smelters will be established once refinery and mines are operating. It remains to be seen where in the state these will be located, and where they will get power and water.

Figure 1: Map Showing the Bauxite Deposits of Andhra Pradesh and Orissa

Source: Map from Rao & Ramam 1979

Note: The Jindal refinery is located close to Kottavalasa and thus very close to the deposits of the Araku group. It is estimated that the Araku Group Mountains could be mined for Jindal for 15 years in which time the more remote but larger deposits of Sapparla could be opened. The railway line shown as ending in Araku has branches north to central Orissa as well as west to present-day Chhattisgarh.

One of the main reasons for the complicated bauxite project setup is the strong protection of tribal land rights in Andhra Pradesh. This earlier prevented the deal between the TDP government and a Dubai company to materialise, and plans had to be finally abandoned in 2003.[39] The present Congress government has learnt from earlier 'mistakes' and signed agreements to mine via a façade government company using, what is referred to as, "raising contractors"[40]. When APMDC does not have the capacity to mine, it will be these raising contractors, privately owned firms, who will hire labourers, own and operate mining equipment, etc. In short, they will do what in common language can be described as to mine. But since the mining lease will be in the name of APMDC, there will be a claim that it is still government-operated.

APMDC will, via the contractors, transport the ore to a

---

39. Between 1999 and 2003, advanced plans to mine bauxite and even amend local land transfer laws were made by the previous TDP government. Ultimately these plans had to be dropped because of major local opposition and campaigns against amending the laws. Recent rallies have seen the TDP claim to have changed its mind completely to now support local people losing land and livelihoods to the projects. Party competition with Congress for the upcoming elections is a more likely reason for the change of opinion, but nevertheless the TDP is expected to mobilise strongly in the future and so are other opposition parties. A number of NGOs and other organisations are also working on the issue but there is very little in terms of a coordinated effort.
40. APMDC, like other state mineral development corporations like the Orissa Mining Corporation, does no or only very minimal mining by staff actually employed by the organisation. Instead, their services consist of applying for mining leases and other bureaucratic clearances, and selecting the most appropriate candidate (often leading to allegations of corruption in the selection process) to do the actual job of unearthing the minerals.

location within the state but outside the Scheduled Areas for the benefit of the private industries being established by JSW Aluminium and ANRAK. The land easiest to acquire, and with the lowest cost for the companies, has been identified as assigned land which is held by the poorest sections of farmers in the state. As with the mines, mainly tribal people and to some extent Dalits are losing their land and forests for industries which will never employ them other than in menial positions.

3.2 Bauxite Processing

Bauxite in Andhra Pradesh exists as caps on top of mountains in Visakhapatnam district at an elevation of 900-1420 m. These bauxite caps range from only a few metres of thickness up to 54 metres at the thickest point of Galikonda Mountain near Araku. Bauxite has been formed in these locations over millions of years under the influence of seasonal heavy monsoon rainfall interspersed with a dry, hot climate. Since bauxite exists as a layer on top of the mountains, there can be no underground mining of bauxite. Open cast mining comes with certain permanent effects since there is a need to completely remove whatever top soil with forest and other vegetation in order to get to the minerals.

Refinery operations consist of grinding the ore into fine particles, mixing it in large containers with caustic soda, and heating the solution so that a white powdery substance, alumina, can be separated from all the other components of the ore. Alumina is an intermediary product mainly passed on to smelter plants to produce the aluminium metal. Since the areas where bauxite deposits are available often do not have the energy required for aluminium smelting, refineries and smelters are often located in different places.

The entire proposed mining area falls under reserve forests such as Narsipatnam and Chintapalli reserve forests for Jerrela (452 hectares of this forest land has so far been applied for in environmental clearances) and Sunkarmetta and Ananthagiri reserve forests in the case of Galikonda and

Raktakonda respectively (using 97.5 hectares and 54.7 hectares of forest land). Much of the area may only be forest by name, but it nevertheless remains to be seen how the mining operations will attempt to restore vegetation after mining is complete.

Table 3: Bauxite Deposits of Andhra Pradesh

Group	*Deposit Size (million tons)*	*Mine Area (hectares)*
Araku Group		
Galikonda	14.5	61
Raktakonda	8.6	42
Chittamgondi	28.5	152
Total Araku	51.6	255
Chintapalli Group		
Sapparla	186.3	1,513.2
Gudem	38.4	263
Jerrela	246.0	1,350
Total Chintapalli	470.7	3,126.2
Gurtedu Group		
(East Godavari)	42.6	180
Total	564.9	3,561.2

Source: "The East Coast Bauxite Deposits of India", *Bulletins of the Geological Survey of India*, Geological Survey of India, 1979, No. 46.

Experts outside of government control attribute the often richly forested slopes of bauxite hills to the mineral itself and its porous water retention capacity.[41] The MoEF on the other hand made a note in the ongoing Supreme Court Niyamgiri mining case stating that mining bauxite would actually help water retention of the mountain (and thus forest growth) by developing cracks from the blasts into which water could seep and remain stored in the mountain.[42] A complete lack of independent evaluation of bauxite mining and its effect

41. Sreedhar, 1995.
42. Ministry of Environment and Forests, 2008.

Bauxite Brief Facts

To produce 1 ton of aluminium requires 1.93 tons of alumina. The alumina in turn requires 2.9 tons of bauxite ore to be mined. Therefore 1 ton of metal aluminium needs 5.6 tons of bauxite ore. The ore not used in the process becomes waste in the 'red mud pond'. One ton of alumina results in 1.2 tons of red mud residue.

If the Andhra Pradesh bauxite deposits of 564 million tons of ore are mined at the rate proposed by the two projects at 3 and 4.5 million tons respectively per year, this would mean that the deposits could last at the most 75 years. Since most commercial mining projects are established with a 30-40 year time frame, it is more likely that the deposits will be mined in a much shorter time by the government inviting yet another company to sign a MoU.

One ton of aluminium requires 13,460 kWh* of energy. In a plant producing 2,50,000 tons of aluminium as the one proposed by ANRAK, this means 3,645,000 MWh of energy per year which is approximately equal to the production of one 500 MW power plant. The power will come from coal, which just like bauxite has its own dangers for the environment, water and local communities living in the mine area. Only in India and China are thermal power plants used for aluminium production. In other countries, the electricity comes either from hydro power, as in Canada and Norway, or from natural gas, as in the Middle East.

The S Kota Jindal alumina refinery will require 8 MGD (million gallons per day) while the ANRAK aluminium complex will use 10 MGD. This makes the calculation for ANRAK with a refinery and a smelter seems very low and seemingly in need of upward revision. Both companies have been promised water from the Polavaram project. There is great uncertainty of when or if at all this water will be made available, and if this means that, at least in the short term, water will have to come from nearby reservoirs instead. The Jindal refinery got its environmental clearance based on water from the Tatipudi reservoir despite frequent promises by the company that it would not take water needed for agriculture.

Source: *Draft Environmental Impact Assessment Report of Integrated Aluminium Complex by ANRAK Aluminium Ltd. 2008, and Draft Environmental Impact Assessment Report of JSW Aluminium, 2007.*

* This is a theoretical estimate from the ANRAK EIA. Currently operating smelters in India are using more energy than this, approximately 14,500 kWh/ton of aluminium.

on water availability, both locally and as part of the watersheds for important rivers like the Goshtani and Sileru, make this an important issue for large areas of coastal Andhra. Bauxite mining has come to be seen largely as a threat to local and regional water sources, but not found much response from governments to date.

The mines planned for AP will be a total of about 3 million tons per year. For a mountain like Galikonda with 24 million tons of total estimated deposits, this would mean operations for only 8 years; but the EIA application made by the government indicates that there are plans to stretch mining operations in the Araku area for slightly longer than this up to about 15 years for each mine. The larger but more remote deposits of Jerrela and Sapparla in GK Veedhi Mandal bordering East Godavari will last longer, but these also cannot be expected to last for more than 30 years. What will happen once the mines close down and the companies go away?

Alumina refineries are often located as close to the mines as possible to reduce transportation costs of millions of tons of minerals. Nalco in Damanjodi has constructed a conveyor belt which leads from the mountain directly to the alumina refinery a few kilometres away. Balco in Korba, Chhattisgarh, is an old facility with high transportation costs of ore via truck from relatively remote locations. Vedanta in Lanjigarh has built its refinery at the very foot of the mountain it is hoping to mine. In the case of AP, no private industry or mine can operate in the agency areas forcing the refineries to be located just outside the agency areas where land is still cheap and transport costs can be kept at a minimum. The S Kota refinery is only one or two kilometres away from the Scheduled Area and less than 10 kms by rail from the Galikonda and Raktakonda deposits. The ANRAK Aluminium complex is planning to rely on trucks for ore since there is no railway in the area and the distance is slightly longer.

The main problem with alumina refineries come from

the massive waste it produces and to which there is no other solution than to dump it in one or several waste ponds with the hope that it will remain there from now to eternity away from people and the environment. What remains after the alumina has been separated from the ore is called red mud from its usually red colour coming from the iron ore. Caustic soda residues will also be an important component; but often overlooked is the vast number of other heavy metals which exist in microgram quantities but, due to their heavy toxicity, will have very severe consequences if they spread to water bodies or via the air.

A study of red mud from Nalco in Odisha revealed how the lead content alone was enough to prevent any plant from growing.[43] A 220 acre section of the plant site has been reserved to store the red mud waste for the Jindal refinery in S Kota. The bottom will be lined with a sheet to prevent

Table 4: Some Important Watersheds and Bauxite Mines

Deposit	*Watershed for River*	*Flows to Important Reservoir*
Araku Group		
Galikonda & Raktakonda	Sarada	Raivada (Visakhapatnam district)
	Goshtani	Tatipudi (Vizianagaram district)
	Chilikala-gedda	Tatipudi (Vizianagaram district) Andra (Vizianagaram district) Meghadri Gedda (Visakhapatnam district)
Chintapalli Group		
Jerrela	Sileru	Upper & Lower Sileru Dams
Gudem	Tandava Nadi	Tandava (Visakhapatnam district)

43. Rao et al., 2000.

seepage into the groundwater, high walls will be built to secure the red mud and water sprinklers will be used to keep the dust from moving with the winds. A visit to Balco's enormous red mud pond in Korba, Chhattisgarh, in 2007 showed walls too low to keep red mud from overflowing the brims during the rains. Red mud had been flowing down the slopes and into nearby streams where women wash clothes. Sprinklers were nowhere to be seen on the dusty top where two boys were using the strong winds to fly kites oblivious to the health hazards they were putting themselves through by choosing this site as a playground.

3.1 AP Government-Jindal South West Bauxite Plans

The MoU signed between the AP government and Jindal South-West of the Jindal Group in 2005 was the first agreement to mine and refine the bauxite ore of Andhra Pradesh of the currently ongoing projects.[44] Jindal South West is part of the Jindal Group, one of India's largest business families originating out of Haryana but now spread across India. Why the company has chosen to invest in aluminium through its newly established subsidiary JSW Aluminium is not clear, but the group is currently moving away from only operating in steel to also cement[45] and energy apart from aluminium. Total aluminium investments in AP should be about 9,000 crores which is only a small part of the total expansion plans of the group in various industries, including massive steel projects. The Jindal Group has strong Congress links with one of the Jindal brothers, Naveen Jindal, being an elected MP for Congress in the Lok Sabha as was his father before him.

44. MoU between GoAP and JSW, 2005.
45. A controversial limestone mining lease was awarded recently by the AP government to JSW Cements in collaboration with Gayatri Cements, a small company who originally applied for the lease. Since mining leases are supposed to be granted on a 'first-come-first-served' basis, it was necessary to manufacture this alliance in order to give the lease to JSW.

3.1.1 Refinery

The refinery was initially to be located at Sabbavaram in Visakhapatnam district, but because of popular protest and high land prices, the project was relocated after an EIA report had been made and a public hearing held. It was announced in April 2007 that the new refinery location was close to S Kota in Vizianagaram district. The new plant site is at the foothills of the Eastern Ghats, just outside the Scheduled Areas, on very fertile lands. Borewell irrigation has become widespread owing to the good groundwater table recharged from nearby Tatipudi reservoir and canals. This allows several crops of paddy or sugar cane every year, plenty of coconut trees and large cashew tree plantations. On June 4, 2007 a new public hearing was held. Environmental clearance was forthcoming a few months later despite a 96% local opposition in December 2007.[46] Hundreds of acres of cashew

46. Meeting notes available on the MoEF website indicate that a discussion was held in October 2007 where the project authorities and the AP government were made to explain how they had accommodated the local opposition in order to get the clearance. Blame was put on outside elements coming to oppose at the hearing and the signatures of the local sarpanches declared that the "real" project-affected people were really in favour. MoEF settled with these assurances and later cleared the project in December 2007. Personal visits to the villages whose land was being taken reveal a complete lack of information to what was going to happen to their land and what form of compensation they were going to get. Further, they had no contact at all with members of the Panchayat. No Gram Sabha meetings had been held and the supposed approval to go ahead with the project by the said Gram Sabhas had thus been manufactured by somebody else. Even Panchayat members other than the sarpanch claimed complete lack of knowledge of any statement approving the project. The local administration and the company work together, those affected can be kept completely in the dark while an official rhetoric of local decision-making and influence is kept.

had already been acquired and cut down in January 2008, barely a month after the environmental clearance and subsequent takeover of land.

The area in S. Kota is strategically chosen since it is right on the railway line which currently transports iron ore from Bailadilla mines in Chhattisgarh to Visakhapatnam port. Bauxite will also be transported on the same railway line if plans come through. The proposed mines in the Araku group are all very close to this location and only some 5 kms from the refinery site. S. Kota is also just outside the Scheduled Area but with a significant local tribal population, with some villages that were never included when the Scheduled Areas were demarcated,[47] and other tribal villages that were displaced when the Tatipudi irrigation reservoir on the Goshtani river was built.

The project area consisting of 1,700 acres (including 220 acres of red mud pond) has been cut with surgical precision to avoid house plots which would raise demands for rehabilitation. The project will take away major portions of agricultural land and the houses of some 40 households, but leave 400 households without any or with significantly reduced landholdings. Most of these households are tribal families without any formal education who will find it very difficult to adjust to life with no agricultural land. Land owned by the rich and educated non-tribal farmers closer to S Kota and those having private land titles have generally not been touched since these sections would be able to offer a lot of resistance and demand high compensation.

Almost the entire proposed project area consists of assigned land. This is land which at some point was given by the government to the poor as a welfare measure, particularly to the people displaced from the Tatipudi reservoir. Assigned land cannot be sold but only passed on

---

47. The AP Fifth Schedule Sadhana Committee has been running a campaign for years to get 891 tribal villages included in the Scheduled Area list of the state.

by inheritance, but many of the current occupiers are not the original titleholders[48] making it easier for the government to take their lands. A recent amendment by the AP government allowed it to take back land it had earlier distributed as assigned land without offering any compensation. The fact that compensation is still offered, however meagre it may be, is claimed to be a sign of a 'benevolent' government, not as a right of the project affected to get compensated. Many villagers witness how government officials were telling them "either you take the compensation money now or we will not give you anything later". There are also cases where the original land owners are appearing to claim money for land they have not cultivated for many years but are still the legal owners of those lands. In such cases, negotiations resulted in a share of the compensation money between the cultivator and the original owner.

Land acquisition is done by taking away agricultural land but not acquiring the houses. Officially only 1 village is displaced, but in reality at least 7-8 villages will lose all or most of its agricultural land leaving them with very few options of what to do to support their families in the future.[49] It seems like the government is keen on keeping the official number of displaced people low and is unwilling to offer rehabilitation to anyone not directly losing a house. Any farming on whatever land remains after land acquisition will become very difficult when living next to a red mud or an ash pond. People who make a living, as for example, agricultural labourers, are not included in any compensation package and are not even counted as project-affected people as long as their houses are not acquired.

The land acquisition is more or less completed except some negotiations with private landowners. Private land is

48. People having assigned land titles will sometimes find that they need to sell land to pay off some debt for example.
49. There has not been any information provided either in the EIA or in other official documents as to who exactly the displaced people are.

bought directly by JSW without government intervention and informal sources mention prices of Rs. 20-25 lakhs per acre as compared to the Rs. 2 lakhs per acre given to farmers with assigned land. The assigned land farmers also get an equal amount as shares, that is Rs. 2 lakhs per acre of land, in the refinery and one job per family according to qualifications.

Water for Industry

The Tadipudi reservoir is only some 2-3 kms from the site, whereas Chilakala gedda, a smaller rivulet, flows from the mountains to the site designated as ash pond. The EIA clearance did not state where the water would come from ignoring this important matter by saying that it will be drawn from Raivada reservoir 25 kms away or other sources designated by the government. The proximity of the reservoir and Chilikala gedda to the project area naturally made local farmers suspect these will be the sources of water. JSW issued a press release stating they would get water from VISCO owned by GVMC (Greater Visakhapatnam Municipal Corporation) through a dedicated pipeline. Municipal councillors in Visakhapatnam protested as the city is already facing shortages. Complicating the matter, an explanation was made that Godavari water brought from Polavaram would be passed on to the Jindal factory. But the Polavaram project is itself under litigation and there is no way of telling when it will come through. And even if it does materialise, there is a reservation already to supply water to farmers who earlier lost water to Visakhapatnam city.

When the environmental clearance letter was released, the discussion returned to where it had begun with Tatipudi reservoir since, despite all these discussions, the clearance was based on the company drawing 8 MGD per day. A new round of media discussions followed with the company denying it will take local water but evidence provided indicated the opposite. It is at present not clear where the water will come from in an area at times facing acute water scarcity, and with urban use, especially with Visakhapatnam city projected to grow dramatically in the future.

3.1.2 Mines

The bauxite mines easiest to exploit are the relatively well-connected mountains of the Araku Group. These are the smaller deposits of the state totalling some 52 million tons of bauxite but are expected to last for the Jindal refinery for 15-18 years. Once these have been mined out, the Sapparla group of hills in the remote western part of the district are planned to be opened. The bauxite hills are located in some pockets of Andhra Pradesh not only notified as Scheduled Area, but actually still predominantly dominated numerically by tribal people. Bagata, Nooka Doora and Kondha Dorra communities among other tribes eke out a living off small farming, MFP collection and increasingly coffee plantations in the hills. The 55,959 people (of which 47,005 are tribal) of Araku Valley Mandal and 44,192 (40,057 tribal) of Ananthagiri Mandal[50] are those living in immediate proximity to the proposed mines. This can be compared to the 400 locally recruited workers who were undergoing training to become bauxite miners.

Mining leases were granted to APMDC in December 2007. Galikonda has deposits of 14.5 million tons of bauxite and Raktakonda 8.6 million tons. The next mountain in line for mining would be Chittamgondi which is right on the border to Odisha. This mountain holds a further 28.5 million tons. The 186 million tons of bauxite available in the remote Sapparla Group of hills would be more than enough to satisfy the needs of Jindal making it seem likely that another company will be invited in addition for a similar MoU once the mines have been cleared. By mining the smaller, but more accessible, hills around Araku, the government is hoping to get the time to establish larger mines in more remote parts of the district.

50. Data from the Census, 2001.

Galikonda and Raktakonda act as the dividers between two important watersheds in coastal Andhra, and the starting points of the Sarada River and the Goshtani River. The former is one of the sources for Raivada reservoir, whereas Goshtani River feeds Tatipudi reservoir. The importance of these rivers to agriculture in water-deficient coastal Andhra has not been addressed by any statements of the government on how water will be managed. Even locally, a tribal village which is now getting significant side incomes from tourists visiting the amazing Katiki waterfall will have a real cause for worry as the source of the waterfall is Raktakonda Mountain. Also importantly, some of the main rivers supporting the water scarce coastal Andhra region originate in these hills. The Goshtani River flows from the hills into the Tadipudi reservoir close to the proposed refinery site.

EIAs have been made for the mines, but these have not yet been presented at public hearings. The reasons behind this delay are not known, but are likely to relate to the uncertainty which has been created in state politics since the death of Chief Minister Rajashekara Reddy in 2009. Additional attention will be on central government ministries, especially the MoEF, for approval of the mines given that Vedanta's bauxite mine was denied by the same Ministry in August 2010.

3.2 AP Government-RAK Bauxite Plans

On February 14, 2007, a MoU was signed between the AP government and Ras al-Khaima (RAK) of the United Arab Emirates. This agreement replicated the setup of the earlier APMDC-JSW MoU; the AP government promised to supply ore via APMDC to an alumina refinery established by the RAK located outside the Scheduled Areas but within the State of Andhra Pradesh. In addition, RAK is obliged to build an aluminium smelter.[51]

51. MoU between GoAP and Government of Ras al-Khaimah, 2007.

Due to the sensitivity of bauxite mining in Andhra Pradesh, the normally media-savvy AP government kept the signing of the RAK MoU quiet to the point that it was presented as a news item in an Andhra daily newspaper a full month after it was actually signed. There are good reasons for the AP Government to attempt to keep its collaboration with RAK away from public debate not only due to the frequently raised issues relating to tribal livelihoods and environmental degradation, but also for what appears to be a project mainly meant to support locally influential politicians rather than the economic development of the state.

RAK is not only a mysterious and unexpected business partner in aluminium with, as far as is known, no previous industrial experience not to mention any experience of aluminium. It does however have a ceramic tiles business in Andhra Pradesh already. As a small, rich kingdom of the Middle East it has money and oil which could be used to invest in and produce aluminium. Many Middle Eastern countries such as Dubai, Oman and Qatar are currently either expanding existing, or investing in new, aluminium smelters fuelled by natural gas and oil. The RAK project is likely to fit into a plan of exporting alumina in the future to an aluminium smelter in the Middle East.

Many Middle Eastern aluminium companies are headed by Indian management, but the precise link leading from RAK to the MoU in Andhra Pradesh seems to be the investment RAK made in 2006 in Penna Cements, owned by Andhra Pradesh Congress party treasurer P. Pratap Reddy. This company was similar to the current AP aluminium project set up as a joint venture with the RAK government. Additional links to Andhra Pradesh comes from the existing RAK investments via companies like Rakindo, a newly formed joint venture in real estate together with Trimex, a baryte mining company with operations in Cuddapah of south Andhra Pradesh. Rakindo claims that it will invest several billion dollars in real estate across India over the next few years. The RAK government is also involved in the 16,800 crore Vadarevu and Nizampatnam Ports and Industrial Corridor (Vanpic) project in Prakasam district.[52]

3.2.1 *Refinery*

The RAK refinery is planned for Makavaripalem of Visakhapatnam district. Since the Jindal project ran into trouble with land acquisition in Sabbavaram and had to shift to a new location, an initial attempt was made to acquire land for an SEZ via the government AP Industry and Infrastructure Corporation (APIIC) which could then be handed over to RAK. Acquiring land for an SEZ is easier for the government since it does not need the same clearances to be able to take away land. It quickly became common knowledge that the land was meant for RAK, but the authorities would continue to refuse to clarify this till the land was already acquired.

Since it is the mines which have been at the focus of civil society protests, the refinery has been able to move ahead and start construction without receiving the close attention as the mines. Even the protests against land acquisition and compensation were side-stepped by the government by using APIIC to acquire land. Land could, in this case, be acquired before the awareness-raising environmental public hearing was held since it was officially meant for an SEZ (Special Economic Zone). An SEZ can contain many different companies and thus need not have a public hearing before land is acquired, and the particular companies operating in

52. Trimex was behind the construction of the Hyderabad International Convention Centre apart from being into baryte export. Headed by Telugu-origin Prasad Koneru and his son Madhu Koneru, the company moved its office to RAK from Chennai due to the close collaboration with the government. Prasad is now Rakindo General Manager, whereas Madhu has been appointed as advisor to the Ras-Al-Khaimah Investment Authority (RAKIA), owned and promoted by the Government of Ras Al-Khaimah.

it have been identified. In this case there was only one unit, ANRAK Aluminium; but the principle nevertheless remained with the result that the land was already in the possession of the government before public protest could gather significant strength. The refinery subsequently received environmental approval in late 2008.

Water for the ANRAK refinery will, as in the case of JSW, be taken from the Polavaram project. The site has however been chosen just next to Yeleru canal making this option seem somewhat more feasible compared to the JSW case where long pipelines will have to be built to transport the water.

The RAK refinery is for 1.5 mtpa with an option to double output.[53] This will naturally involve a doubling of the rate of bauxite mining to provide ore to the refinery. The ANRAK EIA also outlines the construction of an aluminium smelter of 2,50,000 tons per year next to the alumina refinery. Yet, there is no provision for a power plant with capacity for more than the needs of the refinery. The EIA claims the smelter will rely on power from the grid[54] to cover the needs of the smelter in a power-deficient state. Further it seems like a very expensive method for the company since the smelter cannot recover from more than 30 minutes of a power cut. Does this mean that a smelter is not going to be built at present? As in the case of water, no apparent solution is identified in the EIA report.[55]

In 2013 the refinery was completed, but it could not be started since it had no ore. It will now, just like Vedanta's Lanjigarh refinery, have to rely on various imported sources.

3.2.2 *Mines*

The Jerrela group bauxite deposit close to Chintapalli in Visakhapatnam district, containing a total 246 million tons

53. BS Envi Tech, 2008.
54. At other locations in the EIA (e.g. p.34) it is contradictorily stated that power will be generated by the complex for the smelter.
55. BS Envi Tech, 2008.

of bauxite, has been reserved for supply to ANRAK's refinery. These blocks, like other bauxite mountains in Andhra Pradesh, are different from those in Odisha or Chhattisgarh in that the hills are smaller and pointier with thick deposits compared to widespread but thin deposits of the former. This means that mining will move from one mountain top of the Jerrila group to the next with few possibilities to install infrastructure like the conveyor belt as, for example, the Panchpatmali mine of Nalco in Odisha. Instead it seems likely that simple roads will be built to the top of the mountains for trucks to transport ore further increasing forest loss.

Chintapalli is the home of Kondh groups of Adivasis among other communities. It has also for a long time been the base of Naxalite groups, but lately the AP government special police has managed to largely drive these groups across the borders to Chhattisgarh and also to some extent to Odisha. The security situation remains tense however and at any time the Naxalites may return followed by further counter-repression by the government. Local activists of political parties find themselves framed as Naxalites and arrested when mobilising against bauxite in the villages. The prospects for mobilisation in this area remain very difficult.

The difficult terrain, the protesting villagers of the Jerrela area and security concerns have all made surveys and planning for the mines impossible. EIAs were prepared with only minimal interactions or surveys in the immediate area next to Jerrela village, but further away villages were not visited by the environment consultants if newspaper reports are to be believed. In order to make a survey based on actual data, attempts have been made to survey the land, but surveyors have been chased away. Helicopters have been used for aerial survey with activists quickly rushing to any spot where a helicopter is seen landing. At the moment nobody seems to know who actually lives in the wider Jerrela area and what the existing livelihoods and environmental conditions of the area are actually like. Older civil society reports bear witness of a large number of villages in the area established by displaced Odisha Adivasi migrants in recent decades. These villages do not appear in any official records since they live on forest land and do not appear in official statistics. A visit to the area in June 2012 indicated that people continue to live in the area.[56]

The environmental clearance for the Jerrila bauxite mines Blocks 1, 2, 3 and 8 were approved by the MoEF on December 12, 2008 despite the lack of data about ground realities in the EIA reports. The Forest Approval has not been granted however after a delay for many years. In 2014 the mines are yet to be opened, or even make any progress on the ground due to litigation by activists in the National Environmental Appellate Authority in Delhi and significant local protests. Whether the forest clearance will also be forthcoming from the MoEF remains to be seen now that the Ministry has rejected the Niyamgiri bauxite mine just across the border in Orissa.

3.3 Future Deals in Bauxite?

A third of the existing deposits are yet to be signed away, including 42.6 million tons of bauxite in the Gudem group of Visakhapatnam district and parts of Sapparla. Central government-owned NALCO, the country's biggest bauxite miner with major refinery and smelter operations in Odisha, have been in talks for many years,[57] even decades, to be able to establish mines in Andhra Pradesh. At one point an announcement was made by former Minister of State for Mining T Subbarami Reddy that an agreement was close at hand, and the Nalco chairman confirmed this to be true.

56. Oskarsson, 2012.
57. Nalco representatives made a presentation on April 22, 2005 for the Chief Minister according to official meeting minutes, where it stated its willingness to establish facilities in AP, before the MoUs were signed with Jindal South West and RAK (Government of Andhra Pradesh, Industries and Commerce Department, 2005).

Since Nalco has been very profitable, in recent years it has declared its ability to finance the AP project without the need for assistance from the central government. With its proven ability to mine bauxite and produce alumina and aluminium, it is also a much better accomplished company compared to the inexperienced partners chosen by the AP government in JSW and ANRAK. What is even more peculiar is that many of the problems stemming from APMDC acting as benami[58] miner for the companies could have been avoided if an agreement was signed with Nalco instead. Nalco is as much a public sector company as APMDC and could have operated the mines on its own and even had the refinery just next to the mines making the current complicated setup with private industry outside the agency areas and mines in the agency unnecessary.

The profits made by public sector Nalco goes directly to the government, and even though it would be the central government benefiting, potentially a profit-sharing agreement could have been worked out for the benefit of both the state and Centre. With royalties being set very low (see section on benefits from bauxite projects below for more on royalties), income from public operations could have meant a big difference; but apparently the priorities of governments in Andhra Pradesh and Odisha are not for earning money for the public exchequer.

In fact Nalco remains so completely out of favour among the decision-makers who control investment all across India, the company has been forced to attempt expansion abroad instead with plans for a smelter in Qatar, a coal mine in Indonesia and refinery operations in South Africa. It is apparently not enough to deliver large profits directly to the government treasury year after year to keep political and administrative forces interested. At the same time, the major private aluminium companies in India, Hindalco and

58. A benami operation is when acting on behalf of somebody else.

Vedanta, are involved in major investments in the country such as the aluminium smelter of Hindalco at Hirakud dam, Odisha, Vedanta's aluminium smelter in Jharsuguda in Odisha, Vedanta's plans, as discussed above, to mine in Lanjigarh with a refinery next to the mine and its attempts to expand mining in Mainpat in Chhattisgarh. The unwillingness of the AP government, similar to the preference of private industry by the Odisha government, to sign deals with Nalco for further mining leases and instead choosing unknown and untested private companies becomes an interesting comment on where the priorities of current governments lie. To understand why this is the case, it would seem best to make investigations into the personal benefits from these projects coming to the politicians, their relatives and, to some extent, their parties and to the bureaucrats.

3.4 What it Means to be Affected by the Project

According to standard government policy, mining-affected communities are those whose land is directly taken away to be mined. On a recent visit to a working bauxite mine in Chhattisgarh, it was possible to visit a tribal village some 500 metres away from a pit where mining was taking place. The blasting done once a day, the constant digging 24 hours a day, and the increasing number of trucks transporting the ore and subsequent generation of dust had not qualified this village to be seen as mining-affected. Nor had the fact that people, since the introduction of mining, were forced to walk down the hill to the valley below and carry all their water every day made them to be recongised as mining-affected. Since their houses are still intact, they cannot claim to be relocated.

There are villages right on top of bauxite mountains such as Barjhola village on Galikonda and Esogoba village on Raktakonda, but these are in a very clear minority to the vast number of villages surrounding these mountains. These villages will not lose their lands, or at least not most of their land, but they will have to face changes in the water availability, dust and rocks coming down the mountain and a lack of access to common resources. This does not mean that the government will in any way consider them as affected by mining according to the existing policies. There will not be any compensation coming to these villages, nor have they been promised jobs.

Compensation from land acquisition in S. Kota has been similar. Having first identified an area with high incidence of assigned land, compensation was only given to those having the proper government documents to prove they were the owners of the land. Since the area is mainly inhabited by illiterate tribal communities, there are inherent weaknesses in this approach, which the government was of course aware of and ready to exploit in order to implement the project at high speed.

Some villages are people displaced when the Tatipudi reservoir was built in the 1960s. Having already been displaced once, they were given new houses and a plot of land to rebuild their lives in the area later acquired for the Jindal refinery. Many of the people displaced from the dam site were forced to sell the land they received in the new location. The problem is that this cannot be done legally with assigned land creating future legal issues which resulted in poor compensation when the JSW refinery was proposed. The tenure of the new occupants, who in many cases have worked the land for several decades, does not show up in the government records. The situation became even more complicated in a number of cases where the old occupants appeared to claim compensation from land they had not been in possession for decades. The government showed little interest in settling these uncertainties, and in the end, those using the land and those with the legal documents were frequently forced to strike deals to share the compensation money.[59]

---

59. Based on fieldwork visits to S. Kota January-April, 2008.

According to the AP R&R policy, resettlement is not required when acquiring agricultural land; it is only the house plots which make rehabilitation mandatory. This is despite well-known land acquisition problems such as the subsequent increase in prices for new land which means that the compensation is lower than what it will cost to acquire new land. Without the possibility to continue farming in a new location, the options available tend to be very limited for land-losers who have not been to school or been trained in any other profession. At S. Kota, they had not even been to the nearest towns to do manual labour since the lands were good enough for them throughout the year given the proximity of the Tatipudi reservoir. The compensation announced by the company did however promise one job per family, but this will, for most families, work out as Class IV employment doing a menial job in the plant. The land acquisition for ANRAK Aluminium followed the same pattern with agricultural assigned land being acquired but as few house sites as possible.

3.5 Who Benefits from the Bauxite Projects?

As much as those intent on promoting the mineral industry promise development to some of the poorest, citizens' experiences in India show a disturbing trend of increased, rather than reduced poverty in the areas which depend heavily on minerals.[60] Across India, and in the bauxite areas especially, one can see how the areas with the best forests, highest rates of tribal communities and mineral wealth essentially are the same. If one wants to mine bauxite, it will invariably mean affecting tribal communities, cutting down forest and disturbing important watersheds.[61] New positive

60. Bhushan and Zeya Hazra, 2008.
61. Important rivers in other parts of India also originate in bauxite areas like Narmada which starts in Amarkantak on the border of Madhya Pradesh and Chhattisgarh, and Vamsadhara in Niyamgiri of Odisha.

developments are taking place where tribal peoples are getting the right to forest titles under the new Forest Rights Act 2006. But how minerals should be utilised and how to solve the costs of mining in relation to tribal people and forests, has hardly been discussed at all so far outside exclusive elite policy forums heavily influenced by corporate interests.[62]

The AP government wants to attract private investors to the state. As in other states, it wants more than just mines since mining bauxite only gives an income of about Rs. 100 per ton of ore in royalty. Therefore, a company hoping to get bauxite from the state is required to invest in industry. This means, in the first phase, an alumina refinery of 1.4 mtpa (million tonnes per annum) and in the second phase, (once mines have started to operate) an aluminium smelter of 0.25 mtpa. There have never been any details released on what the economic benefits to the state will be from these investments other than the jobs, making these difficult to estimate.

Royalty is the only (official) source of income for the state government from mines, but it has traditionally been set very low by central governments interested in promoting industrialisation which often feeds on minerals like coal, iron and bauxite and also giving higher priority to the profits of PSUs (which are collected by the Centre) like SAIL and Nalco over the state government income. The rate for bauxite royalty is set at 0.40% of the price for aluminium on the London Metal Exchange. At current prices, this means about Rs. 86 per ton of bauxite mined.[63] Assuming a rate of 7.5

62. See, for example, the composition of the committee that framed the new mineral policy first presented in 2006.
63. This is an estimate based on available data since it is not known what the exact rate is of the government. Official data from the London Metal Exchange on July 31, 2008 revealed that aluminium was traded at 2,905 USD per ton (http://www.lme.co.uk/aluminium.asp). This is equal to Rs.121,000 at current exchange rates. The rate is calculated as 0.40% of

million tons mined per year by ANRAK and JSW would give the state government Rs. 64.5 crores per year. It is not known what other sources of direct income might exist for the AP government. There have been attempts to introduce a cess on mineral-bearing lands in addition to the royalty, but this has been held up in the courts in relation to iron ore[64] and oil and gas with unknown implications for bauxite. Income from sales tax and other taxes might be substantial for the refineries, but on the other hand the MoUs promise special tax incentives given to "mega fast track projects". It is currently not known what the combination of taxes and incentives will mean for state income.

Nalco can be used as an existing example of the extreme profitability of bauxite projects in the area. In 2006-07, the company made a profit before tax of Rs. 3,620 crores on gross sales of Rs. 6,515 crores. This is a profit margin of an incredible 56%! From this the central government earned Rs. 574 crores from excise duty, Rs. 1,239 crores in taxes, Rs. 140 crores as dividend (the government owns 87% of the shares and gets dividend from the profits) and Rs. 73 crores in taxes on dividends.[65] A total of Rs. 2,026 crores was transferred to the central government in one year alone, though there is no mention of what the government of Odisha earned.

ANRAK will produce 1 million tons of alumina and 2,50,000 tons of aluminium while Jindal's refinery will make 1.4 million tons of alumina, mainly meant for export markets. Alumina has been sold by Nalco at Rs. 22,500 per ton[66] and

---

the price on the aluminium metal content. Assuming 1 ton of bauxite ore contains 1/5.6 ton of aluminium, the rate then is Rs.86 per ton.

64. The same Brahmani steels accused of undue favours when getting the mining lease at Obulapuram took the government to court over the imposition of a cess of Rs.100 per ton of iron ore in addition to the Rs.20 royalty. http://www.thehindu.com/2007/09/03/stories/2007090360210600.htm
65. Nalco Annual Accounts, 2006-07.
66. Nalco Price List, http://www.nalcoindia.com/PriceCircular/alumina.asp

aluminium at Rs. 145,000 per ton. If the same numbers are used for the proposed AP projects, this gives the production of ANRAK a market value of Rs. 2,250 crores for alumina and Rs. 3,625 crores for aluminium while JSW will make Rs. 3,150 crores worth of alumina. If we assume a more conservative profit margin than Nalco's at 40%, ANRAK will make a profit of Rs. 2,350 crores per year and JSW Rs. 1,260 crores. For JSW the investment of Rs. 4,000 crores will thus be paid off after little more than 3 years of operations. ANRAK's Rs. 7,020 crores investment will be even more profitable with a pay off in less than 3 years.[67]

The price for the bauxite ore sold to JSW and ANRAK will be set by a committee created by the AP Government. The MoUs signed promise a low price 'based on cost of production'.[68] If the market price was used to set the price, the state government would benefit enormously compared to the private industry, but in the MoUs the government has signed away the possibility to make profits on the mining. The ore price remains to be fixed leaving many details unknown of the income from mining. The CEC (Central Empowered Committee) in its 2007 report on the Niyamgiri Supreme Court case suggested a bauxite price which did not reflect any direct or indirect subsidy for the company.[69] It suggested a bauxite price set at 1% of the price of aluminium on the London Metal Exchange, approximately Rs. 1,210 per ton of ore at current prices. Mining 7.5 million tons of bauxite in AP would this way earn the APMDC Rs. 907.5 crores per year. Since APMDC promises to pay 20%[70] of its mining profits to a tribal development fund, it would become very

---

67. The cost of setting up a power plant is not included in the ANRAK calculation and will reduce its profitability.
68. MoU between GoAP and the Government of Ras al-Khaimah, 2007.
69. CEC. 2007.
70. The 20% of profits is in line with the suggestion made in the Samatha Judgement.

important how the price was set if mining was to commence. Further the MoUs propose a small fund of 0.5% of revenue from the industries to be part of a local tribal development fund.[71] At Rs. 3,150 crores turnover for ANRAK, this sum should be Rs. 15.8 crores per year.

The main benefit supposed to reach the communities losing land for mines and refineries are from jobs. It is at present not known how many jobs will be created from the mines. About 400 tribals have been identified by the government from the proposed mining areas and sent for training in the southern Cuddapah district baryte mines officially operated by APMDC but in reality run by contractors related to the then Chief Minister Rajashekhara Reddy. For this, the tribals are given a stipend of Rs. 3,000 per month and a promise of jobs once the mines are cleared. Visits to the villages in the immediate vicinity of the bauxite mountains of Araku Valley made it clear that only one village had sent youth for mine training and that too only a few persons. Other trainees seemed to come from farther away from the actual mine sites which might explain their higher degree of enthusiasm for the work. Highly mechanised mining operations are not likely to employ much more than the 400 currently under training. This can be compared to the almost 1 lakh people of overwhelmingly rural households in only the Araku Valley area. To think mining will offer much of a difference in the local employment situation would be to hope for too much.

Similarly the ANRAK complex, with about 2,000 employees once fully operational, and the Jindal refinery with 750 people employed, cannot be expected to make much of a dent in the local labour markets. In S. Kota Mandal alone where the Jindal refinery is being implemented, the population is 74,413 people. It can even be said that the company is in the process of destroying rather than creating

---

71. See 'MoU between GoAP and the Government of Ras al-Khaimah', 2007 and 'MoU between GoAP and JSW', 2005.

jobs, assuming at least two people from each of the 400 households displaced plus two labourers were working on the land owned before the project came.[72] One person per household owning land will be hired by the company but the labourers will not be.

Important questions remain unanswered for the bauxite projects. There is no doubt that JSW Aluminium will profit from the deal but how are the 400 households displaced from the refinery and those in the immediate area threatened by pollution and increased water scarcity to benefit? Will even the government benefit from taxes collected from the refinery operations and if so will these be spent on improved welfare in the S. Kota area, and in Vizianagaram district? Above all, the profits for private companies are much greater than what the public can hope to recover from the plans, raising concerns about who these projects are planned to benefit.

The 2008 Karnataka elections point towards more direct personal income opportunities from mines, and how these can become very important in state politics. All the major iron ore miners of Bellary have joined politics and the winner turned out to be Gali Janardhan Reddy of the BJP.[73] He was the Tourism Minister for sometime in the BJP government. He is the main investor behind the controversial Obulapuram iron ore mines and Brahmani Steels in Anantapur district.[74]

---

72. This simple example ignores the many other uses for the land now acquired, such as fishing in ponds, collecting minor forest produce, sheep-rearing and other uses of land-giving employment in addition to agriculture.
73. Re-elections were ordered when the earlier coalition government between the Janata Dal and BJP failed on the issue of which party should appoint the Mining Minister and the Infrastructure Minister.
74. Brahmani Steels is another case of an unknown company with strong political connections, like the AP bauxite projects, getting mining leases in favour of an experienced public sector entity. Had Vizag Steel been given the iron ore mines of Anantapur, it would not have been forced as at present to buy ore in the open market at rates many times higher than

Closer to home, it is well-known how former Chief Minister YSR has for many years had a family monopoly on the mining and trade of barytes from Cuddapah. Mining is big business for many of the most influential politicians. Former Minister of State for Mining and Rajya Sabha member T Subbarami Reddy is a major contractor and owner of Gayatri Projects which has in the past had contracts from Nalco. Even though the company is mainly into road construction, he clearly has a personal stake in promoting further investment in mining. Official meeting notes and local responses indicate the keen interest taken to promote the Jindal project, first by the then Commercial Taxes Minister Konathala Ramakrishna, and later as it moved to Vizianagaram district, the then Housing Minister Botcha Satyanarayan. As neither of these two ministers has responsibilities for concerned departments, it is not clear why they are taking this keen interest other than to provide local political support for the project.

For the mines in Araku, is it worth all the mentioned risks to mine bauxite for only 15 years? What will happen to the growing coffee plantations? What will happen to the steadily increasing tourism which attracts people to the scenic surroundings and offers new opportunities for local jobs but only if the scenery remains as beautiful as today? How will the watersheds and the environment be affected? The benefits of watersheds and forests to agriculture over a wide area have not been studied seriously, whereas bauxite can be easily put into a monetary value.

3.6 Conclusion

Industrial projects are promoted as investments for development and increased public good. But closer scrutiny of the details reveal what appears to be narrowly directed benefits going to private companies, most often those with

---

the cost of mining. The profits would have gone directly to the government, but it seems that the political establishment is more interested in making private rather than public profits.

good political connections, while the costs of land loss and environmental costs are born by poor people. The way industrial partners are selected and projects are planned indicate significant opportunities for personal profit by influential politicians and bureaucrats who collaborate closely with the industrialists. This is the only way to explain why the government of Andhra Pradesh repeatedly signs agreements for bauxite projects with inexperienced private industrial partners (such as JSW Aluminium and ANRAK) over publicly held experienced ones (such as NALCO), offering little income for the state, and few employment opportunities or other benefits.

The mining part of the bauxite projects are even more difficult to rationalise than the industry since they are more often than not in tribal areas where poor people living off the land have to be displaced if mining is to commence. Local people cannot be expected to benefit from politically motivated mining projects where the capacity to plan, implement and regulate are under the direct control of those hoping to fund their next election campaign, rather than decision-makers who are accountable to the people living in the Scheduled Areas.

The bauxite projects and its effects on people's livelihoods, water availability, forest destruction and general pollution has generated very wide attention in coastal AP. Any political party now in opposition hoping to move forward in the next elections have had to take up this issue. TDP in a remarkable case of amnesia has made a complete turnaround and claims to now be with the people against bauxite. Smaller parties also take up the issue to the point where bauxite yatras in the hills have become an almost weekly feature where parties 'explain' to the local people what will happen when mines open. NGOs and activists operating in Visakhapatnam as well as across the agency have been active and journalists have covered the issues extensively. Seminars and all-party meetings speak of a very active civil society, and yet the plans are proceeding.

Decades of delayed bauxite projects have taught the government-industry nexus many lessons in how to pursue implementation. Earlier administrations tried to get investors to directly establish industries in the agency and failed. Top management of JSW were earlier with Vedanta who in Odisha mastered "the art" of separating mines from industrial projects thus enabling industry to be established first and used as leverage for mine clearance. Learning is still taking place as evident from the changes made between the JSW and ANRAK projects in terms of land acquisition even before the public hearing.

Despite the intricate planning of the separate mining and refining projects, these have all come to a virtual halt in recent years, apart from the ANRAK refinery. The bauxite mining projects are not officially cancelled, but since no actual progress has been made in years, it appears unlikely that they will start any time soon. Civil society and political opposition protests have coincided with a political crisis in the state with strong demands for a separate Telangana state to put any mining plans off the immediate agenda. At a later time the deposits will however again start to interest politicians and business groups giving a reason for civil society to keep vigilance on the issue and continue to exert pressure.

4

Other Mining

4.1 Small-scale Mining

Small-scale mining is a significant activity in the AP Scheduled Areas which largely goes undetected and therefore tends to operate outside regulations. The law clearly specifies that apart from the need to apply for a mining lease with the state government and fulfil other regulatory requirements similar as in other parts of the state, only a tribal person is allowed to hold the mining lease as well as to operate these mines. Even the government itself has agreed to this principle which could be seen in an advertisement circulated in state newspapers of the *Hindu* and *Sakshi* on March 31, 2008. According to this advertisement, tenders were invited for sand mining along the Sarada, Patala and Goshtani rivers in the Visakhapatnam tribal areas, and only members of the Scheduled Tribes could apply.[75]

There is a small set of educated tribals coming up in the area these days who may have the educational and financial means to apply for mining leases like this one on their own. But a more likely scenario is to have a non-tribal apply for the lease in the name of a tribal person to make the venture

75. A number of small-scale mines have also been closed. The Indian Bureau of Mining lists the closure of one garnet mine and one ceramic clay mine due to their being located in tribal areas (http://ibm.gov.in/Abn_website.html).

seem legitimate. And even if the initial application is properly made by a tribal person, there can be opportunities at a later stage to pass on the lease to some other person who might not be tribal since checks are not going to be as stringent as for the original tender.

An important issue in sand mining is the complete lack of concern for the cumulative impact of different mining activities. Concerns have already been raised that the same rivers, Sarada and Goshtani, will be negatively affected by bauxite mining further up the hills in the catchment area as well as the proposed sand mining. This highlights several problems with mining regulation as it operates today. Firstly, bauxite mining as a major mineral is governed by the central government's Ministry of Mines and Ministry of Environment and Forests, while minor minerals, like sand mining, is dealt with by the concerned state government. There will thus never be even an attempt at a coordinated response to these different kinds of mining to understand the cumulative impact. Secondly, the mining applications are made for each proposed site independently. There is very low likelihood that there will be an understanding of the impact of a large number of quarries, especially for small-scale mining, along the same river for water availability and groundwater changes.

Small-scale mining is also included here as an example of the kind of mining which at times is done by tribal people themselves. One common form of mining is for gems and other semi-precious stones used for various kinds of jewellery. It is a common feature in many hills across the tribal region, but especially in Visakhapatnam, East Godavari and Srikakulam Districts, to find that people have decided to start digging seemingly at random for various precious stones. Sometimes there is simply a small hole in the ground and nothing further has been done, presumably since nothing worthwhile was found. But at other times, the mining continues for years in a completely unregulated way by people who have no experience in digging mining shafts, and secure walls and roof from caving in. Thus the most common way of finding out about the existence of a gemstone mine is when an accident happens claiming the lives of some of its poor workers.

Information gathering on this type of activity is very difficult as very few official statistics exist to verify the actual extent of operations. Often it is believed that mining is induced by the arrival of traders with an interest in uncovering the precious stones. Owing to the informal nature of the mines, controls and regulations are almost non-existent. The experience of gem mining seems to show how it is often just about impossible to try to ban or control mining activities when these can be taken up on a small-scale largely without any tools or equipment by people who live in the area, or just about any person who can convince the local administration to look the other way.

To enable better training and safety, an effort of the Tribal Welfare department of the AP government under the name Tribal Mining Corporation has been to apply for mining leases in the name of tribal cooperatives, and then provide facilities and training to allow the polishing of stones for better sales price. However, this kind of operation has never been supported enough by the government to move beyond a small operation of 7-8 small mines and 1 polishing centre in the East and West Godavari districts, but can be said to be the closest thing which exists towards realising the vision of the Samatha Judgement of enabling tribal cooperatives to use their natural resources for own benefit.

When the department also argued that it should be part of bauxite mining activities for the true benefit of tribal cooperatives, the idea was not accepted by the AP government saying that tribals did not have the skills or the finances to take on such ventures. Since the AP government itself also lacks the necessary skills and finances, the solution was to contract private companies while tribal people were kept completely out of the planning. This way the AP government ensured that not only would tribal people not benefit from the planned activities, but neither would anyone else in the state, including the government.

While some limestone and other mines have been prevented from operating in the Scheduled Areas due to the Samatha Judgement, rock quarries for construction material is another example of mining which can continue. Quarrying can start in any given location within days and continue for at least months and sometimes years, even before the authorities start to react. And even when a proper lease has been applied for, legitimate concerns about worker welfare and the health of those living in the vicinity due to the large amounts of dust which are generated, remain unaddressed.

Another important aspect beyond the tribal/non-tribal divide in small-scale mining is the incidence with which women and children work in these mines. Gender concerns in heavy manual labour are rarely, if ever, acknowledged in official reports. In terms of child labourers, Andhra Pradesh is the second highest in the country with 1.31 million children working in 2001 (down from 1.61 in 1991).[76] Many of these workers will end up in stone quarries[77] though, as with many other aspects of mining in this report, it is difficult to ascertain the extent of this in the Scheduled Areas.

The experience of different kinds of small-scale mining in tribal areas, based on the limited information that is presently available, seems to show that this type of mining often goes under the radar of regulatory agencies as well as the protest movements focusing their work on large-scale displacement and livelihood issues. For both government employees and activists, it is hard to find adequate information on all the different activities which are going on, more or less, haphazardly in these remote regions. For the government, this is seemingly not entirely unintentional since many local bureaucrats and politicians will find significant incomes from allowing these activities to continue.

76. Lahiri-Dutt, 2006.
77. Jayalakshmi, 2005.

Small-scale mining could, in some cases, have offered opportunities for income-generating activities where larger size mining requires investments much beyond the capacity of local people to handle. But often, instead, small-scale mining means dangerous and completely unregulated work initiated by various outside merchants and contractors.

4.2 Limestone

Andhra Pradesh has the biggest deposits of limestone in India, 44% of the total, and produces 40% of total ore. Despite the size of the industry, limestone mining has largely escaped the public protests especially seen for bauxite and uranium mining. Even less attention given to coal mining has not come upon limestone. One reason for the lack of widespread protest is the nature of the industry where each mine is much smaller than, for example, a coal mine or even a bauxite mine. Limestone also does not have the special health problems associated with uranium, though concerns exist for workers' health which should have warranted further examination. Another important reason for the lack of attention given to limestone mining might be due to the locations where mining takes place; primarily in Nalgonda, Kurnool, Cuddapah, Adilabad, Anantapur, Karimnagar, Krishna and Rangareddy districts. Though some of these districts are close to major cities (like Rangareddy or Krishna), most are quite far from urban media (and urban activists) compared to, for example, the planned bauxite mines.

Limestone mining for cement production has, in the past, been a strong mining activity in tribal Andhra Pradesh. The existence today of limestone mining in tribal areas is not widely known. Similarly too manganese and dolomite mining goes on in districts where a significant part is Scheduled.[78] Since a general awareness about the perils of

---

78. Manganese ore exists in Vizianagaram, Srikakulam, Adilabad and Prakasam districts. All these, except Prakasam, have significant tribal populations. Dolomite exists in Khammam and Warangal districts but also in the southern districts of the state.

mining has become widespread in the state and the government has acknowledged how only tribals themselves or the public sector can operate in Scheduled Areas, it will be difficult for these sizeable operations to carry on undetected. For example, in the late 1980s and early 1990s, the government had allowed a number of limestone mines in the Borra caves area of the Visakhapatnam Scheduled Areas. These mines had to be closed due to public pressure, but elsewhere in the state, limestone mines still operate, presumably outside of the Scheduled Areas. But each case is special since the exact borders are only understood by a few. For now, it is assumed that limestone mines do not operate in the Scheduled Areas of the state but further investigations are needed to verify this.

There are strong interests within the government and industry to allow the limestone deposits in the Scheduled Areas to be opened up however. One government note suggesting ways to overcome the Samatha Judgement claimed that 'the [Samatha] judgement further implies that large mineral resources including bauxite and limestone in the State of Andhra Pradesh may never be exploited because mining leases in these areas cannot be given [to] anyone other than the tribals. Similarly, no major industrial investment may never take place in the Scheduled Areas of Andhra Pradesh as the state government will not be able to transfer even its own land to anyone other than tribals for setting up industries'.[79] It will be up to a vigilant civil society to keep track when government intentions are seemingly to open up for mining, whether this is being done through open legislative change, more covertly via a state company facade (like the APMDC) or simply by looking the other way when a mine is opened.

79. Ministry of Mines, 2000.

5

Conclusion

The main form of mining presently ongoing in tribal Andhra Pradesh is undoubtedly coal mining. Yet this displacement-causing, land-intensive form of mining has received much less attention than bauxite, though the latter has not even started. Since the public sector can operate in the tribal areas, there has been no possibility to go to court over coal mining. Even environmental regulations are different to some extent for coal compared to major minerals like bauxite. And the significance of bauxite locations closer to the coast, and especially to the city of Visakhapatnam compared to more remote coal mining areas in Khammam, must surely have some part to play.

If current expansion plans in coal are continued, it is however expected that this will become an issue of major protests in years to come. The lack of capacity of the Singareni Collieries to expand at a pace required by government planners and the subsequent introduction of captive mining by private companies can open up opportunities to litigate. So far, we are only seeing captive mining in Andhra Pradesh by other government entities; however this may only be on paper while a closer investigation on site could reveal the frequent use of private contractors.

In the case of small-scale and limestone mining, private operations are officially not supposed to take place in tribal areas. But there is a significant lack of reliable information on how much actually happens indicating a great need for further research.

Much has been accomplished through civil society pressures on environment, land rights and other issues related to mining in tribal Andhra Pradesh. Unfortunately, government interest is more and more along the lines of increased mining and reduced concern for the displaced or the environmental damage. In order to challenge the government and get a better understanding of what mining actually means, it would thus be necessary to challenge the paradigm of mining as a necessary foundation for economic growth. At the moment, mining is seen as an automatic good even if the government earns limited revenue and in spite of the many costs which are endured by the local people and environments. Local people are somehow supposed to automatically benefit when large mineral deposits are opened up even though they may be losing land and livelihoods and additionally, often not having the education to qualify for the few jobs that mining offers.

References

1. Ajay Kumar, P.S. *Support 7 Days Dharna: Campaign Document by the AP Committee for Non-Scheduled Villages.*
2. Beynon, H., Cox, A.W. and R. Hudson, 2000. *Digging Up Trouble: The Environment, Protest and Opencast Coal Mining*, London: Rivers Oram.
3. Bhushan, C. and M. Zeya Hazra, 2008. *Rich Lands Poor People: Is 'Sustainable' Mining Possible?*, Centre for Science and Environment, New Delhi.
4. BS Envi Tech, 2008. *Draft Environmental Impact Assessment Report of Integrated Aluminium Complex by ANRAK Aluminium at Makavaripalem Mandal, Visakhapatnam District, Andhra Pradesh.*
5. CEC (Central Empowered Committee of the Supreme Court), 2005. *Site Inspection Report of the Fact Finding Committee Regarding its Visit to Orissa from December 18-23, 2004*, New Delhi.
6. CEC (Central Empowered Committee of the Supreme Court), 2007. *Supplementary Report in No. 1324 and No. 1474 Regarding the Alumina Refinery Plant Being Set Up by M/s Vedanta Alumina Ltd.*, New Delhi.
7. Comptroller and Auditor General of India, 2002. *Andhra Pradesh State Audit Report (Commercial) for the Year Ended March 31, 2002*, Government of India. Available at http://www.cag.gov.in/html/cag_reports/andhra/rep_2002/com_chapter_2A.pdf (Accessed on September 16, 2011).
8. Environmental Protection Training and Research Institute, 2007. *Environmental Impact Assessment & Environmental Management Plan for the Proposed Manuguru Open Cast-II*

Extension Project Manuguru Area, Khammam District, Andhra Pradesh (Hyderabad: Environmental Protection Training and Research Institute).

9. Fernandes, W., 2009. "Displacement and Alienation from Common Property Resources" in L. Mehta, ed. *Displaced by Development: Confronting Marginalisation and Gender Injustice*. Sage Publications, New Delhi, pp. 105-132.
10. Gopal, K.R., 1996. *Tribals and Their Health Status*, A.P.H. Pub. Corp., New Delhi.
11. Government of Andhra Pradesh, Irrigation and CAD Department, 2006. *Government Order Ms 119 –Rehabilitation and Resettlement Policy of Government of Andhra Pradesh 2005 - Amendment.*
12. Government of Andhra Pradesh, Irrigation and CAD Department, 2005. *Resettlement and Rehabilitation Policy 2005: For Project Affected Families.*
13. Government of Andhra Pradesh, Irrigation and CAD Department, 2006. *Government Order Ms 119 – Rehabilitation and Resettlement Policy of Government of Andhra Pradesh 2005 - Amendment.*
14. Government of Andhra Pradesh, Industries and Commerce Department, 2005. *Minutes of the Meeting held on April 22, 2005 in the Chambers of Hon'ble Chief Minister on Issues Relating to Grant of Leases for Bauxite.*
15. Guha, R., 2007. "Adivasis, Naxalites and Indian Democracy", *Economic and Political Weekly*, 42(32), p. 3305.
16. Indian Council of Forestry Research and Education (ICFRE), 2008. *Draft Report on Environment Impact Assessment and Environment Management Plan for Jerrila Block I Bauxite Mines, Visakhapatnam District, Andhra Pradesh.*
17. International Energy Agency, 2002. *Coal in the Energy Supply of India*, OECD/IEA, Paris: France.
18. Jayalakshmi, M., 2005. *Artisanal and Small Mines in Andhra Pradesh*, Report Submitted to Communities and Small Mines, World Bank, and The Australian National University.
19. Lahiri-Dutt, Kuntala, 1999. "State, Market and the Crisis in Raniganj Coal Belt", *Economic and Political Weekly*, 34(41): 2952–2956.
20. Lahiri-Dutt, K., 2006. *Gendered Livelihoods in Small Mines and Quarries in India: Living on the Edge*, Rajiv Gandhi Institute for

Contemporary Studies, New Delhi and Australia South Asia Research Centre, Canberra. Available at: http://rspas.anu.edu.au/rmap/projects/_docs/Smallscale-mining.pdf [Accessed January 7, 2010].

21. Laxmaiah, A. et al., 2007. "Diet and Nutritional Status of Tribal Population in ITDA Project Areas of Khammam District, Andhra Pradesh", *Journal of Human Ecology*, 21(2), pp. 79-86.
22. Ministry of Coal, 2004. *Coal Statistics*, Available at http://www.coal.nic.in/welcome.html (Accessed on September 17, 2011).
23. Ministry of Coal, 2005. *The Expert Committee on Road Map for Coal Sector Reforms: Part 1*, Government of India, New Delhi.
24. Ministry of Environment and Forests, 2005, *Lok Sabha Unstarred Question No 2770 Answered on March 21, 2005: Grant of Forest Land for Mining*, Government of India, New Delhi, Available at http://164.100.24.208/lsq14/quest.asp?qref=9731 (Accessed on September 16, 2011).
25. Ministry of Coal, 2011. *Annual Report 2010-11*, Government of India, New Delhi. Viewed on September 17, 2011 (http://www.coal.nic.in/annrep1011.pdf).
26. Ministry of Environment and Forests, 2008. *Note on Bauxite Mining in Orissa: Report on Flora, Fauna, and Impact on Tribal Population*, Government of India, New Delhi.
27. Ministry of Environment and Forests, 2008a. *Environmental Clearance Letter for Manuguru OC-II Opencast Coal Mine Expansion Project July 31, 2008*, Available at http://164.100.194.5:8081/ssdn1/showApprovedletters1994.do?projectCode=No.J-11015/144/2007-IA.II%28M%29 (Accessed on December 27, 2010).
28. Ministry of Environment and Forests, 2008b. *Environmental Clearance Letter for Manuguru Opencast Coal Mine Project Dated October 24, 2008*, Government of India, New Delhi. Available at http://164.100.194.5:8081/ssdn1/show Approvedletters 1994.do?projectCode=No.J-11015/905/2007-IA.II%28M%29 (Accessed on December 27, 2010).
29. Ministry of Environment and Forests, 2009. *Minutes of the 49th Expert Appraisal Committee Meeting Thermal & Coal Mining Held on June 23-24, 2009*, Government of India, New Delhi. Available at http://164.100.194.5:8081/ssdn1/getAgendaMetting MinutesSchedule.do; jsessionid=77A57F5DE972AB6B3

B62800794934438?indCode=THE1Jun%2023,%202009 (Accessed on December 16, 2010).

30. Ministry of Mines, 2000. *Note for Committee of Secretaries Regarding Amendment of the Fifth Schedule to the Constitution of India in the Light of the Samatha Judgement*, Government of India, New Delhi.
31. MoU between GoAP and the Government of Ras al-Khaimah, 2007. Memorandum of Understanding between the Government of Andhra Pradesh and the Government of Ras al-Khaimah, United Arab Emirates signed February 14, 2007.
32. MoU between GoAP and JSW, 2005. Memorandum of Understanding between the Government of Andhra Pradesh and Jindal South West Ltd. signed July 1, 2005.
33. Office of the Registrar General, India. 2001a. *Census of India 2001 – Data Highlights Andhra Pradesh: The Scheduled Tribes*.
34. Oskarsson, Patrik, 2011. *Jobless Openings: The Expansion of Open Cast Coal Mining at the Expense of Rural Livelihoods in the Godavari Valley of Andhra Pradesh*, ActionAid India, Hyderabad, India. Available at http://zweland.net/wp-content/uploads/2012/05/Jobless-Openings-Web.pdf (Accessed on December 5, 2012).
35. Oskarsson, P., 2012. "AnRak Aluminium: Another Vedanta in the Making", *Economic and Political Weekly*, 47(52), 29–33.
36. Rao, V.N., B. Rama Krishna and K. Viswanath, 2000. *Environmental Pollution by Red Mud of Damanjodi, Orissa* in *Environment and Waste Management: Proceedings of National Seminar on Environmental Geology with Special Reference to Waste Management*. Department of Geology, Andhra University, Visakhapatnam, pp. 129-132.
37. Rao, M.G. and P.K. Ramam, 1979. *The East Coast Bauxite Deposits of India*, Geological Survey of India. Kolkata.
38. Rao, S.L., P. Deshingkar and J. Farrington, 2006. "Tribal Land Alienation in Andhra Pradesh: Processes, Impacts and Policy Concerns", *Economic and Political Weekly*, 41(52): 5401–5407.
39. Reddy, M.G., K. Jayalakshmi and A. Goetz, 2006. "Politics of Pro-poor Reform in the Health Sector: Primary Healthcare in Tribal Areas of Visakhapatnam", *Economic and Political Weekly*, 41(5), pp. 419-426.
40. Sarin, M., 2009. "Off the Green Track", *The Tribune*. Available at: http://www.tribuneindia.com/2009/20090802/

spectrum/main1.htm (Accessed September 30, 2009).

41. Shashi, S.S., 1994. *Encyclopaedia of Indian Tribes*, Anmol Publications, New Delhi.
42. Sreedhar, R., 1995. *Impacts of Bauxite Mining and Aluminium Industry in India*, Academy for Mountain Environics, New Delhi.
43. Singareni Collieries, 2009. *Executive Summary for Environmental Public Hearing for the Proposed Jalagam Vengala Rao Opencast-II Coal Mining Project Near Kommepalli Village, Sattupalli Mandal, Khammam District, Andhra Pradesh.*
44. Singareni Collieries, 2008. *Executive Summary of Draft EIA/EMP for the Environmental Public Hearing of the Proposed Kondapuram Underground Mine Near Ramanujavaram Village Manuguru Mandal, Khammam District, AP.*
45. Singareni Collieries, 2006. *Annual Report 2005-06*, Hyderabad: Singareni Collieries.
46. Singareni Collieries, 2005. *Annual Report 2004-05*, Hyderabad: Singareni Collieries.
47. Singareni Collieries, 2010. *Annual Report 2009-10* (Hyderabad: Singareni Collieries).
48. Singareni Collieries, 2011. *Opencast Mining: A Bread Winning Mining Method for SCCL*, Available at http://www.scclmines.com/OpenCast.asp (Accessed on September 12, 2011).
49. Supreme Court of India, 2000. Appeal in the Case of 'Samatha versus the State of Andhra Pradesh and Others'.
50. Supreme Court of India, 1997. Judgement in the Case of 'Samatha versus the State of Andhra Pradesh and Others'.
51. Vimta Labs, 2007. *Rapid Environmental Impact Assessment For the Proposed 1.4 Mtpa Alumina Refinery and Co-generation Plant at Srungavarapu Kota, Vizianagaram District, Andhra Pradesh.*

Annexure – 1

Scheduled Areas in Andhra Pradesh

1) Balmor, Kondnagol, Banal, Bilakas, dharawaram, Appaipali, Rasul Chernvu, Pulechelma, Marlapaya, Burj Gundal, Agarla Penta, Pullaipalli, Dukkan Penta, Bikit Penta, Karkar Penta, Boramachernvu, Yemlapaya, Irlapenta, Mudardi Penta, Terkaldari, Vakaramamidi Penta, Medimankal, Pandiborc, Sangrigundal, Lingabore, Rampur, Appapur, Malapur, Jalal Penta, Piman Penta, Railet, Vetollapalli, Patur Bayal, Bhavi Penta, Naradi Penta, Tapasi Penta, Chandragupta, Ullukatrevu, Timmareddipalli, Sarlapalli, Tatigundal, Elpamaehena, Koman Penta, Kollam Penta, Mananur, Macharam, Malhamamdi, Venketeshwarla Bhavi, Amrabad, Tirmalapur, Upnootola, Madhavanpalli, Jangamreddi Palli, Pedra, Venkeshwaram, Chitlamkunta, Lachmapur, Udmela, Mared, Ippalpalli, Maddimadag, Akkaram, Ainol, Siddapur, Bamanpalli, Ganpura and Manewarpalli villages of Achempeth taluk of Mahbubnagar district.
2) Malai Borgava, Ankapur, Jamul Dhari, Lokari, Vanket, Tantoli, Sitagondi, Burnoor, Navgaon, Pipal Dari, Pardi Buzurg, Yapalguda, Chinchughat, Vankoli, Kanpa, Avasoda Burki, Malkapur, Jaree, Palsi Buzurg, Arli Khurd, Nandgaon, Vaghapur, Palsikurd, Lingee, Kaphar Deni, Ratnapur, Kosai, Umari, Madanapur, Ambugaon, Ruyadee, Sakanapur, Daigaon, Kaslapur, Dorlee, Sahaij, Sangvee, Khogdoor, Kobai, Ponala, Chaprala, Mangrol, Kopa Argune, Soankhas, Khidki, Khasalakurd, Khasalabuzurg, Jamni, Borgaon, Sayedpur, Khara, Lohara, Marigaon, Chichdari, Khanapur, Kandala, Tipa, Hati Ghota, Karond Kurd, Karoni Buzurg, Singapur, Buranpur, Nagrala, Bodad, Chandpelli, Peetgain, Yekori,

Sadarpur, Varoor, Rohar, Takli and Ramkham villages of Adilabad taluk of Adilabad district.

3) Ambari, Bodri, Chikli, Kamtala, Ghoti, Mandw, Maregaon, Malborgaon, Patoda, Dahigaon, Domandhari, Darsangi, Digri, Sindgi, Kanakwari, Kopra, Malakwadi, Nispur, Yenda, Pipalgaon, Bulja, Varoli, Anji, Bhimpur Sirmeti, Karla, Kothari, Gokunda, Gogarwudi, Malkapur, Dhonora, Rampur, Patri, Porodhi, Boath, Darsangi, Norgaon, Unrsi, Godi, Sauarkher, Naikwadi, Sarkani, Wajhera, Mardap, Anjenkher, Gondwarsa, Pipalsendha, Jurur, Minki, Tulsi, Machauder Pardhi, Murli, Takri, Parsa, Warsa, Umra, Ashta, Hingni, Timapur, Wajra, Wanola, Patsonda, Dhanora, Sakur and Digri villages of Kinwat taluk of Adilabad district.

4) Hatnur, Wakri, Pardhi, Kartanada, Serlapalli, Neradi-konda, Daligaon, Kuntala, Venkatapur, Hasanpur, Surdapur, Polmamda, Balhanpur, Dharampuri, Gokonda, Bhotai, Korsekal, Patnapur, Tejapur, Guruj, Khahdiguda, Rajurwadi, Ispur, Ghanpur, Jaterla, Khantegaon, Sauri, Ichora, Mutnur, Gudi Hatnur, Talamedee, Gerjam, Chincholi, Sirchelma, Mankapur, Narsapur, Harkapur, Dhampur, Nigni, Ajhar Wajhar, Chintalbori, Chintakarvia, Rampur, Gangapur and Gayatpalli villages of Boath taluk of Adilabad district.

5) All villages of Utnur taluk of Adilabad district.

The Scheduled Area in the State of Andhra Pradesh were originally specified by the Scheduled Areas (Part A States) Order, 1950 (C.O.No.9) dated January 23, 1950 and the Scheduled Areas (Part B States) Order, 1950 (C.O.No.26) dated December 7, 1950 and have been modified vide the Madras Scheduled Areas (Cesser) Order 1951 (C.O. 50) and the Andhra Scheduled Areas (Cesser) Order, 1955 (C.O.30).

6) Rajampet, Gunjala, Indhani, Samela, Tejapur, Kannargaon, Kantaguda, Shankepalli, Jamuldhari, Gundi, Chorpalli, Saleguda, Wadiguda, Savati, Dhaba, Chopanguda, Nimgaon, Khirdi, Metapipri, Sakra, Sangi, Devurpalli, Khotara-Ringanghat, Nishani, Kota Parandoli, Mesapur, Goigaon, Dhanora, Pardha, Surdapur, Kerineri Murkilonki, Devapur, Chinta Karra, Iheri, Ara, Dasnapur, Kapri, Belgaon, Sirasgaon, Moar, Wadam, Dhamriguda, Dallanpur, Chalwardi, Ihoreghat, Balijhari, Sakamgundi, Ara, Uppal Naugaon, Anksorpur, Chirakunta, Illipita Dorli, Mandrumera,

Dantanpalli, Deodurg, Tunpalli, Dhagleshwar, Padibanda, Tamrin, Malangundi, Kandan Moar, Geonena, Kuteda, Tilani, Kanepelli, Bordoum Telundi, Maugi Lodiguda, Moindagudipet, Chinnedari, Koitelundi, Madura, Devaiguda, Areguda, Gardepalli, Takepalli, Choutepalli, Rane Kannepalli, Sungapur, Rala Samkepalli, Chopri, Doda Arjuni, Serwai, Rapalli, Tekamandwa and Meta Arjuni villages of Asaifabad taluk of Adilabad district.

7) Gudam, Kasipet, Dandepalli, Chelampeta, Rajampet, Mutiempet, Venkatapur, Rali, Kauwal, Tarapet, Devapur, Gathapalli, Rotepalli, Mandamari, Dharmaraopet Venkatapur, Chintaguda and Mutiempalli villages of Lakshetipet taluk of Adilabad district.

8) Bendwi, Chincholi, Goigaon, Hirapur, Sakri, Balapur, Manoli, Antargaon, Wirur, Dongargaon, Timbervai, Sersi, Badora, Vmarjeeri, Lakarkot, Frgaon, Kirdi, Sondo, Devara, Khorpana, Kanargaon, Chenai, Kairgaon, Samalhira, Dhanoli, Marnagondi, Yellapur, Katalbori, Isapur, Devti, Panderwani, Wansari, Perda, Wargaon Nokari, Mirapur, Pardhi, Kutoda, Parsewara, Mangalhra, Karki, Nokari, Manoli, Sonapur, Inapur, Mangi, Uparwai, Tutta, Lakmapur, Kirdi, Injapur, Jamni, Hargaon, Chikli, Patan, Kosundi, Kotara and Sonorli villages of Rajura taluk of Adilabad district.

9) Ralapet, Kistampet, Takalapalli, Chakalpalli, Anaram, Bhepalli, Korsni Isgaon, Chintaguda, Ankora, Usurampalli, Arpalli, Bophalpatnam, Balasaga, Pardhi, Tumrihati, Chintalmanopalli, Chintam, Gullatalodi, Damda, Dhorpalli, Kanki Garlapet, Gudlabori, Gurmpet, Lomveli, Mogurdagar, Wirdandi and Chilpurdubor villages of Sirpur taluk of Adilabad district.

10) Kannaiguda, Ankannaguda, Raghavpatnam, Medarmiola, Koetla, Parsa Nagaram, Muthapur, Motlaguda, Venglapur, Yelpak, Kaneboenpalli, Medaram, Kondred, Chintaguda, Kondaparthi, Yelsethipalli, Allvammarighunpur, Rampur, Malkapalli, Chettial, Bhupathipur, Gangaram, Kannaiguda, Rajannapet, Bhutaram, Akkela, Sirvapur, Gangaram Bhupathipur, Pumbapur, Rampur, Ankampalli, Kamaram, Kamsettigudam, Ashnaguda, Yellapur, Allaguda, Narsapur, Puschapur, Bhattupalli, Lavnal, Vadduguda, Kothur, Pegdapalli, Srvapur, Bhussapur, Chelvai, Rangapur

Govindraopet, Ballapali, Dhumpallaguda, Kelapalli, Lakhanavaram, Pasra, Gonepalli, Padgapur Govindraopet, Ballapali, Dhumpallaguda, Kelapalli, Lakhanavaram, Pasra, Gonepalli, Padgapur, Narlapur, Kalvapalli, Uratam, Kondia, Maliat, Aclapur, Dodla, Kamaram, Tadvai, Boodiguda, Bannaji, Bandam, Selpak, Kantalpalli, Sarvai, Gangaguda, Tupalkalguda, Akulvari, Ghanpur, Shahpalli, Gagpelli, Chinna-beonnplli, Venkatapur, Narsapur, Anvaram, Lingal, Ballepalli, Bandal and Thunmapur villages of Mulug taluk of Warrangal district.

11) Vebelli, Polara, Bakkachintaphad, Ganjad, Thirmalguda, Gopalpur, Khistapur, Tatinari Venpalli, Pattal Bhoopati, Chandelapur, Battalpalli, Advarampet, Satiahnagar, Dutla, Mothwada, Mangalawarpet, Karlai, Arkalkunta, Kodsapet, Gunderpalli, Masami, Battavartigudem, Mamidigudam, Pangonda, Roturai, Satreddipalli, Konapur, Kondapuram, Pogulapalli, Govindapuram, Makadapalli, Peddalapalli, Yerravaram, Kundapalli Neelampalli Daravarinampalli, Karnegund, Mahadevagudem, Marrigudem, Jangalpalli, Bavarguda, Oarbak, Gangaramam, Mucherla Amaroncha, Kamaraam, Chintagudem, Nilavancha, Kangargidda, Madagudem, Dalurpet, Kothagudem, Kotapalli, Goarur, Radhiapur, Gazalgudem, Rajvepalli and Bollypalli villages of Narsampet taluk of Warrangal district.

12) All the villages of Yellandu taluk of Warrangal district (excluding the Yellandu, Singareni and Sirpur villages and the town of Kothaguda)

13) (i)All the villages of Palocha taluk of Warrangal district excluding Palondha, Borgampad, Ashwaraopet, Dammapet, Kuknur and Nelipak villages and (ii) Samasthan of Paloncha

14) Visakhapatnam Agency area 1 (excluding the areas comprised in the villages of Agency Lakshmipuram, Chidikada, Konkasingi, Kumarapuram, Krishnadevipeta, Pichigantiko-thagudem, Golugondapeta, Gunupudi, Gummudukonda, Sarabhupalapatnam, Vadurupalli, Pedajaggampeta) 2 (Sarabhupathi Agraharam, Ramachandrarajupeta Agraharam, and Kondavatipudi Agraharam in Visakhapatnam district).

15) East Godavari Agency area 2 (excluding the area comprised in the village of Ramachandrapuram including its hamlet Purushothapatnam in the East Godavari district).

16) West Godavari Agency area in West Godavari district.

1. Inserted by the Madras Scheduled Areas (Cesser) Order, 1951
2. Inserted by the Andhra Scheduled Areas (Cesser) Order, 1955

Source: Ministry of Tribal Affairs, Government of India. Available at http://www.tribal.gov.in/Content/ScheduledAreasinAndhraPradeshSSAreas.aspx(Footnotes)

Annexure - 2

Singareni Collieries Expansion Plans

Table 1: Summary of Forestry Cases Pending as on December 15, 2009

Project	*Extent in Ha*	*Present Status*
First Renewal of GK OCP (Phase-1)	261.31	to issue formal approval for reduced extent.
Kunavaram OCP	21.09	to submit consent of Gram Sabha.
JVR OCP-I (Expn)	136.5	to issue demand for submitting of compliance report.
Khairaguda OCP Expansion	126.71	to issue demand for submitting of compliance report.
Bellampalli OC-II Extn. B&D Blocks.	108.78	to issue first stage approval.
Second Renewal of Kothagudem ML	1174.18	to issue GO.
Dorli OCP-II(Phase-II)	26.90	to submit report on FR Act.
Third Renewal of North Godavari ML	1105.0	to issue first stage approval / to issue demand for submitting of compliance report on TWP
RK OCP (Phase-I)	202.50	to forward the proposal to GOAP.
Manuguru OCP	33.58	to forward the proposal to GOAP.
JVR OCP-II	776.20	to forward the proposal to CF, KMM
Abbapur OCP	165.92	to forward the proposal to GOAP.
Kondapuram Mining Lease.	477.03	to issue first stage approval.
RG OCP-II Expn	147.42	to forward the revised proposal to CF, WGL.

Incline entries for Kondapuram UG Mine	10.50	to forward the proposal to CF, KMM.
Kistaram OCP	285.44	to forward the proposal to DFO, KMM for scrutiny and re-submission.
Total	**5059.06**	

Source: Singareni Colleries website, http://scclmines.com/cpp/fi.doc [Accessed 2010-01-06]
OCP = Open Cast Mine
UG = Underground Mine

Table 2: Summary of Mining Lease Cases Pending as on December 15, 2009

Project	*Extent in Ha*	*Present Status*
Kunavaram OCP ML	60.48	to submit clarification on period of lease for applied area.
First Renewal of Bhoopalpalli ML	2792.0	to issue GO.
Third Renewal of North Godavari Mining lease.	4494.0	to forward the application to DMG with addl. Information.
Dorli OCP-II (Phase-II) ML	26.90	to forward the application to DMG.
Kondapuram Mining Lease	477.03	to issue prior approval.
Addl. Mining Lease for Manuguru OCP	373.90	to issue prior approval.
Sand Mining Lease Near Gumpenapalli and Ganapavaram (Vgs.)	116.25	to forward the application to DMG.
First Renewal of Chennur ML	1683.0	to forward the application to DMG.
Total	10023.56	

Source: Singareni Colleries website, http://scclmines.com/cpp/fi.doc [Accessed 2010-01-06]

Table 3: Singareni New Open Cast Projects

Project	*Schedule of Preparation*
Peddapur OCP Phase-I	September 2009
RK-5&6 OCP(RKP OC-II)	September 2009
MNG OCP-II Extension (Phase-II)	December 2009
Mahadevpur OCP	December 2009
KTK-6 Phase II OC	February 2010
MNG OC Extension	March 2010
Goleti 1&1A OC	March 2010

Table 4: Singareni New Underground Projects

Project	*Schedule of Preparation*
KTK-3 Incline (Longwall)	Under process
Sravanapalli I UG	Under process
Laxmidevipet	Under process
RKP SB I UG	October 2009
Sravanapalli II UG	September 2009
KTK-9 Incline	October 2009
RKP SB II UG	December 2009
Chennur 5 Incline	November 2009
Chennur 6 Incline	January 2009
Chennur 7 Incline	February 2009
MM Shaft Block (sector-D&E)	January 2010
MM Shaft Block (sector-B)	January 2010

Table 5: Ongoing Projects at Singareni Colleries

Project	*Type of Mine**	*Capacity (MTY)*
Adriyala Shaft Project	UG	2.144
Shanthi Khani Longwall Project	UG	1.167
Jallaram Shaft Project	UG	2.285
Kakatiya Longwall Project	UG	2.747
Kakatiyakhani - 6 Incline	UG	0.312
Kondapuram	UG	0.510
Vakilpalli-BG	UG	0.490
VK 7 Continuous Miner	UG	0.400
Continuous Miner at GDK-11A Incline	UG	0.400

Semi-mechanisation with Diesel Operated LHDs in GDK-5 Inc UG	0.450	
Khairagura OCP/ RFR	OC	0.72/ 2.50
Dorli OCP-I	OC	0.700
Dorli OCP-II	OC	0.700
Koyagudem OC-II	OC	2.000
Srirampur OC-II	OC	2.500
Abbapur OCP	OC	0.600
JK 5 OCP	OC	2.000
Sravanapally OCP	OC	2.000
Indaram OCP	OC	1.200
Medapalli OCP Expansion	OC	3.000
Manuguru OC-II Extension	OC	4.000
RG OC-I Expansion Phase-II	OC	1.500
RG OC-III Extension	OC	4.300
KTK OC Sector -I Project	OC	1.250
Manuguru OC Project	OC	1.500
Total		**38.2+**

* Underground or Open Cast mine
Source: Singareni Colleries website
+ Excluding the uncertain number for the Khairagura mine